THE
BONES
OF BIRKA

Unraveling the Mystery of a
Female Viking Warrior

C. M. SURRISI

CHICAGO
REVIEW
PRESS

Copyright © 2023 by C. M. Surrisi
All rights reserved
First hardcover edition published in 2023
First paperback edition published in 2024
Published by Chicago Review Press Incorporated
814 North Franklin Street
Chicago, Illinois 60610
ISBN 978-0-89733-260-6

The Library of Congress has cataloged the hardcover edition under the
following Control Number: 2022951946

Cover design: Preston Pisellini
Front cover image: Evald Hansen, WikiCommons
Back cover image: Tancredi Valeri, courtesy of Neil Price
Interior design: Jonathan Hahn

Printed in the United States of America

This book is dedicated to the person who was buried in grave Bj 581. It's been over a thousand years since they put you in there, laid you out, and prepared you for the afterlife, and over one hundred years since others removed the rock and began scrutinizing your situation. You have been so many things in the minds of so many people. You have been the subject of research, academic articles, documentaries, fictionalized movies, and novels. You have stirred imaginations, inspired hope, and started brawls on blogs. By all accounts, if those were your weapons, you had one heck of a violent life. I don't think the people who buried you imagined that your afterlife would lead to your being the subject of this book. In some ways I am sad about the scrutiny your old bones have gotten. In other ways I am uplifted and feel great promise for your contribution to our understandings of Birka, Vikings, Eastern trade, and, well . . . humanity. I wish I knew your name, but I don't think I would have wanted to meet you in the flesh. I'd say rest in peace, but I know that's not possible.

Then the high-born lady saw them play the wounding game,
she resolved on a hard course and flung off her cloak;
she took a naked sword and fought for her kinsmen's lives,
she was handy at fighting, wherever she aimed her blows.

—*The Greenlandic Poem of Atli*, stanza 49
(translated by Carolyne Larrington, 1996)

CONTENTS

1

A REMARKABLE FIND: BIRKA, SWEDEN, 1878

IMAGINE IT'S 1878 on the island of Björkö, in Sweden's vast Lake Mälaren. A bug scientist, Hjalmar Stolpe, has hired a few local farmers and trained them, on the job, to **excavate** graves. He calls them his "professors."

Stolpe originally came to Björkö, which means Birch Island, looking for insects encased in nuggets of ancient **amber**, but instead he stumbled onto much, much more—the one-thousand-year-old Viking town of Birka.

With tools in hand, the men are set to open one of the island's over three thousand graves. Stolpe takes out his notebook and writes "Bj" for the town of Birka and "581," for the grave number. Bj 581 is in a prominent position and has a spectacular lake view.

Erik, Stolpe's lead excavator, lifts his hat and scratches his head. The other excavators lean on their shovel handles. There's one giant problem: a boulder looms in the middle of the grave. They'd grappled with such stones before, but none quite so big. Some stones stood straight up, and others were egg-shaped and lay on their sides, but this one is a puzzler. It's tall enough to be seen from a distance, and it's a full eight feet across.

They shake their heads at the idea they might roll it, so they launch into the next best thing: they start digging around it. After steady progress pitching their blades into the earth and scooping out soil, the point of a shovel pierces through material that was once wooden beams. They all crowd around and drop to their knees. Erik directs them to brush the earth away carefully with their hands.

Soon their efforts reward them with a view of the end of a sizeable chamber grave and the promise of what might be inside it. The excavators murmur excitedly. Applying all the methods they've been taught, they carefully, tediously, broom and brush the earth away from the wooden walls. It's slow going, and they don't rush it. After all, whatever is in this grave has been there for a very long time. There is no harm in being careful.

With the enormous rock still blocking the center of the grave, the excavators decide to explore the end and its contents. With even greater caution, they clear the layers of dirt and debris that have fallen into the mortuary home of a Viking who once walked these grassy hills.

The men crouch down as they work, thin layer by thin layer, until . . . wait . . . part of a bone shows itself. Then another. And another. Working painstakingly, shaving through the soil, they meticulously expose a skeleton from the depths of the late **Iron Age** to the year 1878.

Stolpe's eyes explore the skeleton. Its four legs are bent into a tight tuck. Close to it is another in the same posture. The two are packed together on a ledge that spans the end of the chamber. Stolpe's pulse quickens. This is significant. Two horses. Two. Someone important lies within this grave. Stolpe has great hope for a significant find inside.

He steps back and ponders the boulder that hinders their ability to meet the Viking who lies below it. His mind runs through the options.

Before they do anything more drastic, the men fashion wooden levers and lodge them under the rock to try to pry it loose. They try various positions and angles. They grunt. They push. They shove. All to no avail.

It's a dilemma, but then again, Stolpe is a master of solving problems. He decides they will break up the rock with controlled blasting so as not to harm what's under it. Of course, feeble efforts won't suffice either. They must use just the right amount of dynamite to keep from blowing the rock, the grave, and what's in it to smithereens.

Being as careful as they can be with dynamite, they begin to disassemble the rock, chunking it into smaller and smaller bits until they can clear it away entirely. It's a slow and dusty endeavor. But when they finally reach the grave, remove remaining bits of fallen rock, and carefully excavate the contents, what appears before them is nothing short of remarkable—even for men who have already opened over five hundred other Viking graves.

Stolpe uses quarter-inch graph paper to draw an image of what he sees. He measures the dimensions carefully and finds the overall wooden, room-like chamber grave to be 5.9 feet deep, 11.5 feet long, and 5.5 feet wide. He draws in the 2-foot-by-3-foot ledge at the eastern end that holds the well-preserved and complete skeletons of the two horses, showing them next to each other on their stomachs.

Then he begins memorializing something that has never been seen before in any Viking grave. He draws the skeleton of a person that lies on its side. It looks to him as if it had been seated when placed in the chamber. Accompanying the person are two shields, one sword, and a very long knife in a leather sheath with a richly embellished mounting of gilded bronze.

That's not all. He continues to sketch. There are twenty-seven game pieces and three dice of bone in the person's lap. A game board accompanies the game pieces. There is a bronze dish, in which lies a small iron spear with a silver-plated socket. There is a knife and a whetstone. There is a battle-ax and a variety of arrows. There are stirrups, buckles, parts of bridles, a large horse comb of bone, and a variety of iron fittings for harnesses or saddles.

That's not all. His hand moves across the checked graph paper, recording items in their relative positions. Next to the corpse's head

lies a cone-shaped ornament of silver embellished with fine orna-
mental wire in a lacelike pattern known as *filigree*. It looks to be a
decoration for the peak of a cap made of cloth. Fragments of glass
are scattered around the remains of a jacket along with four large
tufts of silver thread.

Stolpe is ecstatic. He believes he may have uncovered one of the
most significant graves in all of Scandinavia. When he completes
the inventory and has sketched of all the items in the grave, he
records in his **field research** notes that he has excavated the grave
of a warrior. His mind must be racing over the significance of the
find and how it will raise his prestige and secure his position and
funding. In this moment he might feel like he is the king of the
archaeological world. He wouldn't be wrong. He will eventually be
called the "King of Birka."

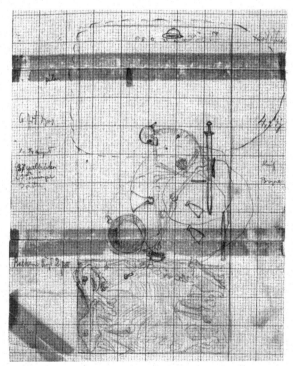

Stolpe's fine-drawn plan of Bj 581. This is the primary visual record of its
disposition, made during excavation in 1878.
Swedish History Museum/SHM (CC BY)

2

WHAT WE KNOW
ABOUT THE VIKINGS

THE VIKING PEOPLE CAME from what are today's Denmark, Norway, and Sweden, but they knew no national boundaries or geographic borders. The people we call Vikings did not include all Norse or Scandinavian people. Neither could the word be used to describe a culture. They have been consistently described as bloodthirsty pirates. And while they were indeed seafaring explorers who raided, plundered, and traded in human beings as slaves, they were also families, farmers, shipbuilders, peaceable goods traders, talented craftspeople, skilled poets, and much more.

In Old Norse, the word *víkingr* translated roughly as "pirate." According to the written descriptions from the Viking age, a víkingr was a man who has gone away on a journey to raid or for military purposes, usually in a group. We know that women also went on these voyages. The word was not necessarily always associated with violence, since the people also engaged in trading. They were most commonly called Northmen, Danes, pagans, **Rus**, *vaeringjar*, *Majus*, and a host of other names. In reality, it depended on whom you asked—which *culture* you asked. *Rus*, for example, was originally the term for Scandinavians who visited and settled in what is now called Russia; it is thought that the Finnish word for a Swede,

Ruotsi, may have derived from it. And *Majus* is the Arabic word for *them*, meaning "fire worshippers," technically applied to members of the Zoroastrian religion but in practice used for any pagans and non-Muslims who weren't obviously Christian. It is also thought to be connected to the name of people from a particular region on the Swedish east coast, *Roslagen*—"rowers" or "people who row."

Many Viking trading towns existed, including Kaupang in Norway; on Gotland, Sweden's largest island; Hedeby, in Denmark; and Birka, Sweden. Hedeby may have been the largest, but Birka, on an island in Sweden's Lake Mälaren, was one of the most notable. People from remote northern locations brought raw materials into Birka, where they were used to produce jewelry, textiles, and other goods, which were in turn taken on trading voyages to distant lands. Their metalwork, woodwork, and art were highly developed and showed superior craftsmanship. Birka, like a number of these towns, was heavily fortified. Trading stations along the rivers and waterways, where traders became settlers, were set up to protect the trade routes.

The Vikings did not have a religion as we think of it today with a bible, Torah, or set of rules and creed. They had a belief system that

Map of Viking world expansion.
Max Naylor, Wikimedia Commons

included pagan gods and a fluid concept of life and life after death. Their beliefs were woven into their daily existence and contained elements of superstition, magic, and shamanism. Near the end of the Viking Age, Christianity was adopted as an official religion. They also told stories and listened to poems to impart knowledge and learn right from wrong.

Many history books mark the Viking Age from two key events in English history: the raid at Lindisfarne island off the coast of Northumberland in 793 CE through the Battle of Stamford Bridge in Yorkshire in 1066 CE. But it's not that exact. Think of it more as a period of transition beginning around 750 CE (plus or minus a couple of decades) and winding down earlier than 1066 CE.

Before 750 CE, Vikings both traded peaceably with Europeans and engaged in wars among themselves. Their transition to marauding and pirating through the territories of thirty-seven present-day countries and with over fifty cultures has not been fully explained. Many reasons have been suggested, including a desire for settlement on more favorable agricultural land, a backlash to Christianity, and a voracious desire for wealth and perpetuation of their power and lifestyle.

The Viking Time Line

1–400 CE	Scandinavian warriors become a respected social class.
600–800	Kingdoms are formed. Birka trading center established.
789	Sporadic Viking attacks on England occur.
793	Vikings brutally raid and pillage the Lindisfarne monastery.
799	Vikings attack Aquitaine, and Charlemagne prepares fortifications.

834	The *Oseberg* Viking ship burial of two women.
829-830	Ansgar makes his first Christian mission to Birka.
840-841	Vikings first remain in Ireland for the cold months, and settlers establish Dublin.
842	Vikings first remain in Francia for the cold months.
844	Vikings attack Seville, Spain.
845	Vikings raid and plunder Hamburg, Germany, and Paris, Francia.
850	Vikings first remain in England for the cold months.
859-862	Björn Ironside and Hastein raid towns along the Mediterranean coast.
860	Vikings plunder Constantinople (Istanbul, Turkey).
862	Russian town Novgorod is founded by Ulrich.
866	Vikings establish presence at York, England.
870-930	Vikings settle Iceland.
871	Alfred the Great, king of Wessex, stops Viking inroads.
872	Harald I takes over Norway.
879	Rurik establishes Kyiv.
886	Danelaw Pact divides England between Alfred and the Vikings.
911	Vikings establish Normandy in France.
941	Vikings attack Constantinople.
954	Eric Bloodaxe ousted from York.
981	Erik the Red lands in Greenland.
986	Viking ships venture into Newfoundland waters.
991	Æthelred II pays ransom to stop Viking attacks on England.
995	Olav I conquers Norway.

1000	Christian missionaries reach Greenland and Iceland.
1000	Leif Eriksson, son of Erik the Red, explores the coast of North America.
1000	Olav I dies; Norway is ruled by the Danes.
1002	Brian Boru ends Viking domination of Ireland and becomes king.
1010	Thorfinn Karlsefni attempts to found a Viking settlement in North America.
1013	Canute the Great (also Cnut or Knut), King of Denmark becomes King of England.
1015	Vikings abandon the Vinland settlement in North America.
1028	Canute conquers Norway.
1050	City of Oslo is founded.
1066	The Battle of Stamford Bridge, which is often considered the end of the Viking Age.
1079	Final Viking invasion of England.
1179	Poet and historian Snorri Sturluson is born.
c. 1220	The Prose Edda is written down by Snorri Sturluson.
c. 1270	The Poetic Edda is compiled.

VIKING BOATS

The design of Viking boats was core to the Vikings' success as travelers. Their longboats or longships had shallow bottoms, or **drafts**. They were initially designed to navigate the stretches of creeks, rivers, lakes, deep sea inlets, and brackish bays swirling around the many Scandinavian islands, without bumping into rocks and logs.

When the Vikings ventured out into the harsh Northern sea, their ships required something to keep them from tipping over, so they invented the keel, a blade that extended downward approximately forty inches from the bottom of the ship. The keel enhanced stability, increased speed, and allowed for masts and sails by creating balance. With a keel the ship could have easy passage as a rowing boat along the rivers of Rus territory (Russia) and also handle the demands of an open, restless sea. The keel also provided for easier steering, and masts and sails enabled speed.

Would you want to go on a Viking voyage? Maybe not. The ships were open deck and crowded with barrels, drinking water, trading goods, and sometimes animals. Each person had a sea chest or bag, but the sea could be bitterly cold and it was not unimaginable that two people would sleep together for warmth. There were no toilets, and everyone relieved themselves over the side of the ship. Because of the size of the ship and the crowding, this couldn't be done in private, and because of the waves, this couldn't be done alone. It required a partner to hold on to you so you didn't fall overboard. Close quarters may have spawned squabbling. Vikings infrequently bathed or washed their clothing, if they did it at all, and illness was likely not treatable. Even their sophisticated navigation, which got them to their destinations faster, would not have been much consolation for the misery of the journey.

Fleet of Viking long ships, by Danish artist Alfred Larson (1860–1946).
PD-US Wikimedia Commons

VIKING SOCIETY

Vast social and economic differences existed in Viking society.

Slaves

It should not be ignored or minimized that slaves were one of the Vikings' most significant trading commodities. Slaves were people who were captured in battle, hunted after a raid, or born into slavery. Additionally, some crimes were punished by enslavement. The town of Hedeby had an internationally known slave market where Christian missionaries reported seeing their peers displayed for sale.

Thrall is one Viking word for *slave*. The Vikings also used the words *ambátt, bryti, fostri/fostra, deigis*, and others, which related to gender, country of origin, and other identifications. The lives of slaves were dire, and while it was possible for them to be freed, they were most often treated brutally and as less than human.

Freemen

Freemen were the largest part of Viking society. Apart from those in the aristocracy, they included farmers, landowners, leaseholders, hunters, stablemen, shipbuilders, merchants, professional warriors, bodyguards, craftspeople, and traders. Not all freemen owned the land they farmed. Agriculture was the basic occupation. Freemen had the right to express their views at the Thing (the Assembly) where public matters were aired. They also had both a right and a duty to carry weapons.

Women

While there is evidence that men had the upper hand, there is also a strong belief that Viking women exercised considerable power and authority and were respected members of their own segment of the social order. After all, someone had to run the community while the men were away on trading and raiding voyages. Sources tell of women running farms, raising families, and engaging in the home crafts of needlework, spinning, and weaving. Women are also associated with paganism and shamanism.

Some descriptions of Viking exploits include women as warriors on raids, dead on battlefields in warrior gear, and as wives on settlements abroad. Women were often traded or sold into marriage by their fathers but were able to seek divorce from abusive husbands.

Children

Viking childhood was brief. From an early age, children were given tasks to do and as much responsibility as they could handle. From the earliest days of their lives, children learned that life was hard, brutal, and bloody and that survival didn't come easy. There was no "childhood" as we know it today. Children who grew up in a trading town like Birka would see people from all over the world. With war and aggression a permanent part of their lives, they probably looked at the warriors as heroes and wanted to follow in their footsteps. Children were indoctrinated into Viking ideals by being told tales of gods, monsters, giants, kings, and warriors. The mystique of these stories spun by the hearth prepared them for their own heroic adventures.

Kings and Nobility

Kings got their power from the gods, or so they claimed, and they passed it along to their descendants. Thus, a dead king was succeeded by his son, but there was no fixed order. He could pick whichever one he wanted, and that often produced a lot of fighting among siblings. Sometimes, the squabble was resolved by splitting up the kingdom. Kings were surrounded by jarls, or earls, who were their trusted confidants (and were also oftentimes their enemies and those who unseated them). Kings had vast power. They owned or controlled large swaths of land and animals, had the right to inherit land, and had the right to collect tribute and taxes. Some women were included in nobility, mostly by marriage and birth. Kings and nobility oversaw freemen, women, children, and slaves.

Viking communities initially had separate leadership, and rivalry existed among them, causing fierce clan wars. Kingdoms rose and were attacked, but ultimately the entire Viking world was never unified. Tales of Viking leaders included King Harald Fairhair, who united Norway; Canute the Great of Denmark, England, and Norway; Eric Bloodaxe of Norway and York; Harald Klak of Denmark; Svein Forkbeard of Denmark; Rollo, duke of Normandy; Ivar the Boneless; and Leif Eriksson.

RAIDING AND TRADING

According to law, Viking men were expected to be community defenders, and they could be full-time or part-time warriors. They were required to possess weapons and were fined if they failed to do so. They could join a dedicated group of warriors called a *band*, guard the home front, sign up to go on a raid, trade, or do any combination of these things. They were free agents. Sometimes they worked as mercenaries, going to war for money rather than loyalty to king or country.

Vikings traded furs, hides, bird feathers, whale bones, walrus tusks, ropes, weapons, jewelry, weavings, utensils, and other crafted goods. It is also known that a large component of their trading was in people—thralls, or slaves. Traders accompanied warriors on raiding ships, and warriors accompanied traders for protection. Traders often had a scale for weighing currency in one hand and a sword or knife in the other. A trader might dress in the style of people he was trading with, and even though he didn't speak the language could easily discern value for goods. Scholars indicate that women were on both raiding and trading voyages.

Good sailing ships and expert seamanship allowed Vikings to travel vast distances. They arrived as pirates, traders, extortioners of tribute, mercenaries, conquerors, rulers, warriors, emigrating farmers, and colonizers. Their impact was felt throughout Europe, the Middle East, and North Africa, and as far west as Iceland, Greenland, and North America. Some even say their reach extended into China. Their voyages in easterly directions generally involved populated lands, battles, settlements, and political intrigue. Their voyages to the west were generally to sparsely populated lands and became efforts to settle and establish farms. This was the case with Iceland, Greenland, the Faroes, and North America. In North America, however, they were met with a hostile reception from indigenous peoples who vigorously resisted them. The Vikings eventually abandoned their efforts and left.

REDISCOVERING THE VIKINGS

Even though the Viking Age ended one thousand years ago, these extraordinary people are not out of mind or out of sight. Tales of their exploits were recorded by their victims and they themselves told stories of their exploits which were handed down in the oral tradition and eventually written down. And as **archaeologists** do, soon there were excavations of Viking towns.

One Viking trading town, Birka, which flourished for approximately two hundred years, was abandoned in the 970s CE for reasons that are not clear. By the 1800s it was nothing more than an island of grassy mounds, below which lay the remains of thousands of Vikings.

In 1871, a young scientist named Hjalmar Stolpe set foot on the island to do geological studies, not knowing what lay beneath his feet. After making a few **bore holes**, he unexpectedly uncovered one of the most significant Viking finds in history. His journey to fully explore Birka wasn't easy. It took many years and academic and political battles. Eventually, he made one of the most significant finds of all Viking **archaeology** and would become known as the King of Birka.

3

HJALMAR STOLPE:
THE KING OF BIRKA AND HIS
MOST FASCINATING FIND

HJALMAR STOLPE HAD A REPUTATION for being meticulous, determined, and passionate long before he was standing at the precipice of grave Bj 581 in 1878.

Imagine a young Stolpe foraging in the undergrowth of his family backyard. Dirt grinds into his knees, and sweat drips from his forehead. He drags himself stealthily on his belly by his elbows to capture the illusive Swedish insect, the *Neuropterida*. Once he focuses on his prey, he strikes with lightning speed. Then with muddy shoes, he bolts from the yard to the house and up to his room to record and categorize his new specimen. He ignores a call to dinner as he pens a letter to a scientific implement manufacturer inquiring after special needles, forceps, and microscopes.

Like almost every kid, Stolpe liked some school subjects better than others, but his father, Justice Mayor Carl Johan Stolpe, was a stern man with high expectations of his son. Luckily, Hjalmar's scores in the natural sciences were not merely high but the highest possible. His grades in math, Latin, and philosophy paled by comparison. His father wasn't entirely pleased, but he still doted on his clever and determined son.

Stolpe's enthusiasm for insects didn't wane as he grew up—it only increased. He attended Uppsala University, where he studied ants and became an entomologist. His papers included skillful drawings. He painstakingly took hours to draw his ant subjects— every detail of their eyes, sharp claws, antennae, and mandibles were all inked into this work. In his graduate paper, he passionately argued the importance of investigating ancient insects encased in fossilized tree resin called *amber*.

As a passionate entomologist holding degrees in zoology and botany, he researched where amber was located so that he might find some and examine it for ancient insects. He learned that some amber had been found in a rich, black-dirt area of an island not far from Stockholm. The island was Björkö, and it was only a boat ride away.

On Tuesday, October 3, 1871, Hjalmar Stolpe, now age thirty, stepped onto a boat and took the two-hour ride west of Stockholm to Lake Mälaren, which is a large bay of the Baltic Sea. The lake is

Map designed by Chris Erichsen Cartography.

made up of numerous arms that encircle many islands and jutting peninsulas. Stolpe was headed for one of those islands: Björkö.

Björkö is only a few square miles in size, and the only inhabitants were a small number of farmers whose families had worked the land for generations. Stolpe likely paced the deck as the boat approached the island and itched to get his hands into its black dirt to find amber.

Stolpe had packed equipment he used as a student, including the standard geological hammer, spade, and stick drill. He brought

Hjalmar Stolpe.
Swedish History Museum/SHM (CC BY)

along very little clothing, not expecting to be there for a long time. But he did have notebooks to record his finds.

Almost immediately after the boat docked, Stolpe jumped off and began to explore the island. The next day, he strolled along the beach making the first entries into his diary. He wrote of finding cones, wood, charcoal, bits of tree, hazelnuts, and cherry kernels. He happily noted, "A small piece of amber!"

Soon he found this process too slow and turned from foraging and scraping the earth to drilling bore holes. He made lists in his notebooks, documenting the exact places he had dug (including the farmers' potato fields), and he made his first sketches. Little did he know these notebooks and sketches would change archaeology forever.

Stolpe may have been the first bug scientist on the island, but he wasn't the first scientist to poke around there. In the early 1800s, Johan Hadorph, the Swedish director of the Central Board of National Antiquities, dug in the soil. Two or three graves had been excavated by F. W. Brannius in 1811, and thirteen graves had been investigated by Alexander Seton in 1825–1827. One physician, Anders Blad, reported finding "a multitude of strangely cut beads from amber, oriental carnelian, and other noble stones." But none of the others saw what Stolpe saw.

Because ancient graves had been previously identified on the island, there was an ordinance for the protection of the "remnants of prehistoric living areas." It required a permit to dig in locations that might contain ancient remains. But Stolpe ignored this. He was exploring the Black Earth area that had no visible signs of human remains or relics, so he powered ahead with his hole boring without seeking a permit.

He wasn't exactly free to do what he wanted, though. Some scientists back in Stockholm—members of the Royal Swedish Academy of Sciences—backed Stolpe, but many experts at the rival organization, the Royal Swedish Academy of Letters, History, and Antiquities, did not. They considered him a rank amateur, a nonarchaeologist, and they kept their eyes on him.

Björkö may have been an island with a lot of black dirt, but all that black dirt, it turned out, was the site of Birka, an important Viking Age trading town mentioned in several medieval literary and historical sources. And Stolpe's boreholes were making Birka a political hot potato.

Royal Academies

The Royal Swedish Academy of Sciences (the "Academy of Sciences") is a nongovernmental scientific organization founded in 1739 to promote the natural sciences and mathematics. Each year it awards the Nobel Prizes in physics and chemistry.

The Royal Swedish Academy of Letters, History, and Antiquities (the "Antiquities Academy") is the academy for the humanities founded in 1753 by Swedish Queen Louisa Ulrica. Among its many publications is the historical journal *Fornvännen*.

Even though he was being observed by the watchdogs of the country's monuments, Stolpe continued digging, and he found many more interesting things than amber. Soon he requested, and was eventually given, official permission to dig within a specified area.

With further digging, Stolpe ultimately concluded that the amber that he was finding through dredging the harbor had been dropped from Viking ships into the sea when they were unloading a cargo of amber from East Prussia and not amber that was original to Birka's black dirt. As for the amber bits found in the soil, he believed they were also remnants of trade connections between Birka and the people around the Baltic. So Birka ceased being about amber for Stolpe, and he pressed on to uncover the Viking town.

Not only did he grab on to the expanded project with zeal, he also enlisted the help of local farmers, training them to be archaeological excavators. He called them his "professors."

One fine day, he was rewarded with the discovery of an Iron Age refuse heap. He jubilantly wrote to his father about it:

> I dug for two days in "Black Earth" and dug six feet deep down to the varved clay and then 8½ feet with a drill. . . . The remarkable finding during these digs was a layer of bones five feet thick! Full of bones! Ox, swine, sheep, pike, hare, fowl or waterbirds, worked [carved] horn of Elk, etc. Iron fragments were found at a depth of 4 or 5 feet. My interpretation is that I was digging in a refuse heap [or kitchen midden] from the Iron Age.

He also wrote to his father that he wanted to bring some of his finds back to Stockholm to show the Academy of Sciences, but he needed a few things before the trip. He explained he'd been prudently doing all his digging in his nightshirt so that he would still have a clean day shirt:

> I must ask for a wool sweater, a pair of underpants, a nightshirt, and a pair of wool socks immediately. Keep in mind I have been digging in **black** earth! Since I have been wearing my nightshirt during the day this whole time on Björkö, I already have a clean day shirt.

It is hard to imagine that Stolpe had been doing all his excavating with only two shirts, one meant for the day and one he typically wore at night, and that he had even saved the day shirt for a trip back to Stockholm. He was happily enduring considerable discomfort and a lot of handwashing for his Birka passion.

Stolpe proudly made the presentation in Stockholm in front of many important people and felt he had made a good impression, but he got into all kinds of hot water over his use of one word.

During his presentation, Stolpe had described the garbage dump as a "kitchen midden," and that, his enemies accused, was a gigantic mistake. They said any professional archaeologist should know *kitchen midden* was a **Stone Age** term, not an Iron Age term. They said his use of the term could mislead people about the date of the Birka find. One of his loudest critics, Hans Hildebrand, wrote, "Only someone so inexperienced would use that term."

The attack stung Stolpe. It also infuriated him. One word! His pride in his precision had been wounded. He fumed about it and wouldn't let it go. However, his personal notes and correspondence suggested he recognized the problem with the term. He had used "kitchen midden" (*kjökkenmödding*) when he meant "garbage dump" (*avskrädeshög*). And now there was a push among academics to *not* accept him as an archaeologist.

But Hjalmar Stolpe rose above it and showed what he was made of. He accepted that he needed to be a credentialed archaeologist to have academic standing at Birka, but he also felt archaeology needed to up its game by incorporating more science. He formulated a plan to make both of these things happen.

STOLPE PROMOTES A "NEW ARCHAEOLOGY" AND BECOMES A "REAL" ARCHAEOLOGIST

Stolpe turned his efforts to promoting the advancement of what he called the "new archaeology." He wrote, "I am convinced the only archaeology that has a future is that which supports itself in natural science." He also began academic work on his doctorate degree in archaeology with the same thesis in mind.

Members of the Academy of Sciences loved Stolpe and his image for advancement of a "new" archaeology. He branded himself as a man of the future, one with natural science experience and a documented interest in archaeology who was headed in the "right" direction. They supported him and his plan to fully take over responsibility for Birka.

Stolpe put his efforts into writing a PhD dissertation and then acquiring the necessary approvals. With the help of his supporters, he was able to get the glowing reviews and approvals needed, not only from scientists but also from leading classical archaeologists. Once he had the credential of archaeologist, it was decided Stolpe would be the one and only leader of the Birka investigation.

Stolpe was earning his nickname of the King of Birka. He continued his excavations with zeal, and perhaps his background in entomology and geology was the best thing that could have happened to this site. As an entomologist he was precise in his categorization, and as a geologist he used his knowledge of scrutinizing earth and rock layer by layer, called *stratigraphy*, which produced careful examination.

In his journal for 1872, Stolpe provides a list of the equipment he needed out on the island: bone brushes and old toothbrushes, glue, slippers, cummerbund, shaving kit, box of paints, medical supplies, a copy of the Gerss Björkö map from 1826, measuring tape, a brass handle for a pair of water goggles . . . a sandwich box, cigar box, flypaper, shells, percussion caps, and the alcoholic beverages *brännvin* (Rånäs) and sherry. Thereafter come notes about a dinner, with Swedish explorer Baron Nordenskiöld among the guests, who are served pork, Swedish punch (*arrack*), and beer.

Stolpe pioneered a digging technique that was an archaeological innovation for the Swedes. Stratigraphy had not been used in archaeology.

> Instead of a more or less random dig where things looked promising—the way Stolpe had dug the first year—he made strictly measured areas where the workers methodically dug themselves down. The result was long, narrow dikes/pits, so-called trenches, which length could vary between fifty and one hundred meters, between one and three meters wide and about two meters deep. Much importance was placed on the pit wall profiles [depth and steepness] being cleanly polished. The piles of earth that were thrown up between the dikes had certainly been investigated but this did not fulfill the demand. . . .

"I have been compelled an uncountable number of times during the digs in the Black earth to have the workers again go through a whole pile of turned-over earth to find a fragment of an object that had been damaged while digging it up. Such a 'punishment dig,' as it was surely considered by the workers, was just as important to keep the object as intact as possible, as for the sake of the discipline. I could not let the workers believe that we let the excavations proceed unmethodically."

In a report to the Academy of Sciences on January 8, 1873, he describes how the earth was carefully scanned, shovel for shovel, and how he applied a systematic and detailed examination and recording method to even the smallest item, so that small finds like "beads as well as fish bones could be collected, drawn, and placed into paper envelopes."

Stratigraphy

Stratigraphy (or the process of stratification) is the layering of soil and debris on top of one another over time. The lower layers are older, and the higher layers are newer. Carefully exposing the layers and preserving and examining each can help an archaeologist determine the sequence of events. They call this the "law of superposition." Many things can confuse the interpretation, such as post holes, rodent burrows, erosion, and other disturbances to the natural layers. Archaeologists are particularly concerned with things that are in the layers that can be attributed to human behavior, like artifacts. Artifacts can help archaeologists date the layers and more precisely understand what occurred in that spot years ago, sometimes thousands of years ago.

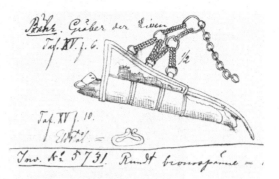

Image from a Stolpe
notebook, 1875.
Swedish History Museum/
SHM (CC BY)

The method was revolutionary in archaeology. It received international attention with the Anthropological-Archaeological World Congress.

Stolpe made scaled drawings on graph paper with squares of one-tenth of a *decimaltum* (approximately 0.97 inch, or about 25 mm). He also appreciated the need to excavate an entire burial mound, not merely the center of it.

In 1875, he wrote in a letter to Hans Hildebrand, "I investigate the whole mound, leaving nothing unexcavated, and therefore often find several burials in one mound."

Over time his number of notebooks grew and eventually became an encyclopedia of the dig. They contain detailed drawings of graves, his comments, findings, measurements, archaeological data, and other valuable information.

His team grew. He employed not only more local men but also a young woman who worked at the site as an illustrator, and he even gave his daughter a role. With the help of his team, he uncovered cemeteries that encircled a town where seven hundred to one thousand Viking people once lived over a period of two hundred years.

He numbered graves, recorded their condition with drawings and field notes, and carefully managed the contents, called **grave goods**. Not surprisingly, Stolpe treated source material with exacting standards. He recorded the names of each workman responsible for excavating each grave. Eriksson ("Erik"), Stolpe's lead excavator, or "head man," also recorded particulars in thirteen notebooks.

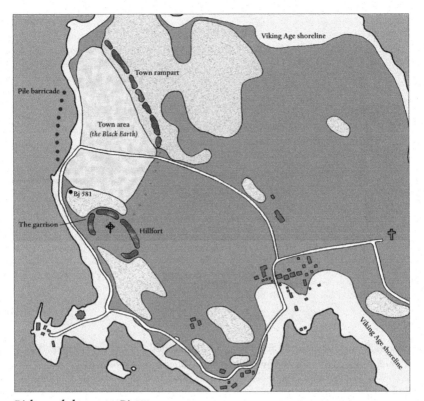

Birka and the grave Bj 581.

BJ 581: THE MOST FASCINATING GRAVE IN BIRKA

Then came the day in 1878, when Erik dug beneath one of the large granite boulders at a high point on the site and history was made. After the workmen went through a painstaking process of removing a giant boulder from atop the grave and excavating the chamber, grave number Bj 581 revealed the body of what Stolpe interpreted as a high-ranking, male Viking warrior and his impressive weapons and other grave goods.

He took meticulous notes, made detailed drawings, and collected and stored the bones by grave number. Stolpe's interpretation was that the person was a high-ranking warrior from the 900s CE. Over time, Stolpe assessed the **context** and contents of the grave and came to remarkable conclusions.

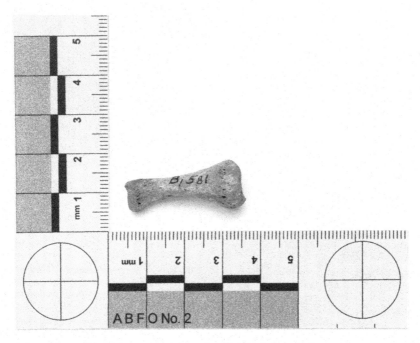

A bone from the skeleton in Bj 581, clearly labeled with this provenance; all elements of the surviving postcranial skeleton bear identical documentation. *Photo: Ola Myrin, Swedish History Museum/SHM (CC BY)*

The Size and Location of the Grave

Grave Bj 581 was sited on a high point overlooking the water, harbor, and town and could be seen from the town and the water. Its large memorial stone, if that's what it was, would have caught the eye from a distance. It was even higher in elevation than the two graves near it that also contained numerous weapons. This position was between the more elevated **hillfort** and the lower situated **garrison**. The grave was built of logs and measured 11.5 feet by 5.5 feet and 5.9 feet deep. This would be approximately the size of a commercial dumpster. Also, Stolpe had learned from the experience of opening other graves that the boulder suggested high social rank or military service—the person was likely a defender of Birka.

In addition to Stolpe's original drawing, there are three other drawings of the grave and its contents.

Harald Olsson's drawing of Bj 581, based on Stolpe's field records.
Olsson's image was used by Holger Arbman in his primary report in 1943.
Swedish History Museum/SHM (CC BY)

An engraving of Bj 581 made in 1889 by Evald Hansen. Produced for an article in *Ny Illustrerad Tidning* in 1889, the image gives us a lively impression of the grave, but for the small details Hansen consulted Stolpe's original drawing. *Evalo Hansen / Wikimedia Commons*

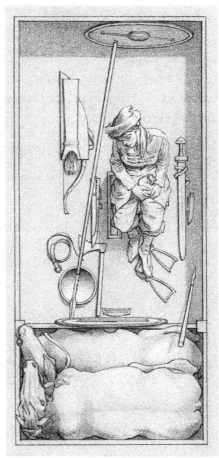

Representation of chamber grave
Bj 581 as it may have looked
when the grave was closed.
*Drawing by Þórhallur Þráinsson, © Neil
Price. Courtesy of Neil Price*

The Person in the Grave

The grave contained a single body with most of the bones intact. The person appeared to have been seated initially but had fallen to the side as the body deteriorated. It was Stolpe's opinion, which he noted in the journal for Bj 581, that bodies in chamber graves were usually seated.

"In the center of the chamber the dead warrior seems to have been seated on a low chair. It is difficult to explain this strange position of the skeleton in any other way, and other finds demonstrate that the dead were usually seated in such chambers."

The Weapons Were Splendid

There was a full complement of weapons in Bj 581. The type, diversity, and volume of weapons suggested to Stolpe they belonged to a working military person of high rank and distinction: a sword, ax, fighting knife, two lances, two shields, and twenty-five armor-piercing arrows.

Stolpe's team unearthed in Bj 581, among other things, a sword, battle-ax, fighting knife, two lances, two shields, and twenty-five armor-piercing arrows. *Photo: Christer Åhlin. Swedish History Museum/SHM (CC-CY)*

Hnefatafl

In addition to the weapons, the skeleton in the grave held a bag with the pieces needed for playing a game of strategy. Stolpe described the bag as holding three weights, three dice, twenty-seven game pieces, including a "King piece," and a collection of angled pieces of iron that may have formed a game board. The game, known to archaeologists as *hnefatafl*, was a Viking game similar to chess. Anyone could play the game, but those of higher or privileged status might have had higher-quality pieces, and being a good player was itself a mark of refinement. Some experts have linked the game to military strategy and say it indicates the person had a knowledge of military tactics. Along with the weapons and horses, the game suggested the find of a significant military man. There have been similar finds in other burials of elites.

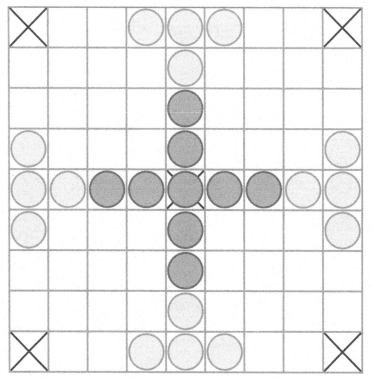

Hnefatafl board with pieces.

According to archaeologist Leszek Gardeła, "Furthermore, it is clear from Old Norse literature that playing strategy games, such as *hnefatafl*, was not only a strictly male activity—several women stemming from different social strata are portrayed in extant sources as actively engaging in this pastime. . . . There are some textual hints, however, implying that the ability to play games was among the skills nobles were required to master." To illustrate the point, Gardeła points to this twelfth-century poem by Earl Rögnvaldr of Orkney:

> I am quick at playing chess,
> I have nine skills,
> I hardly forget runes,
> I am often at either a book or craftsmanship.
> I am able to glide on skis,
> I shoot and row so it makes a difference,
> I understand both the playing of the harp and poetry.

Some of the *hnefatafl* pieces found in Bj 581.
Swedish History Museum/SHM (CC BY)

The Horses

Finding a horse skeleton in a Viking grave was not unusual, but finding two horse skeletons was extraordinary, as they were reserved for higher ranking warriors. And finding the skeletons of a stallion and a mare was even more unusual. Their presence signaled the importance of this person, as warriors needed their horses in their graves so they could travel with them to *Valhöll*, the Hall of the Slain, in Norse mythology. Near the horse skeletons were four ice crampons, or snowshoes for horse hooves. There was also a comb made of antler that was so large that Stolpe believed it had to be a currycomb for the horses.

The Clothing

Remnants of the person's clothing survived. They were from imported silk textiles embroidered with silver brocade. The cloth looked to be from the **Eurasian Steppe**, an area of grassland extending from modern-day Hungary through Ukraine and Central Asia to Manchuria in northeastern China. This is an area that Vikings were known to travel to on raids and for trade. It wasn't clear to Stolpe whether these items were manufactured in Birka or acquired on travels abroad, but he was convinced they were the property of a high-ranking warrior, since only such an individual would have such objects in connection with the weapons and horses in the grave.

The Hat, Pin, and Buckles

Along with the clothing, Stolpe and his team found forty tiny fragments of mirrored glass on the ground of the grave as well as a simple ring-shaped pin of iron near the skeleton's shoulder. A silver-trimmed cap of luxurious silk with an unusual silver tassel was also found, as were four plum-shaped, granulated silver balls. Some experts believe they hung from the tassel. Others say they may have been attached to other parts of the cap. A miniature spearhead with a hole pierced through it seemed to have been used as a pendant.

Tassels, buckle, and pins from grave Bj 581.
Photo: Christer Åhlin. Swedish History Museum/SHM (CC-BY)

What Was NOT in the Grave

Many books on Vikings describe their graves in terms of stories passed down through the ages, such as burial by burning in a boat if the person was high ranking, but one of the hallmarks of Viking funeral ritual is that almost every grave was unique in its details.

Bj 581 was no exception. It contained an array of items that Stolpe associated with the profession of warrior. That did not mean that a sword, spear, or ax hasn't been found in other, "nonwarrior" graves, but in this one there was an unusual assemblage. In addition, there were no grave goods that Stolpe would have associated with typical female cultural roles, such as jewelry, weaving tools, and keys. To him, the evidence weighed in favor of a warrior grave, which without hesitation, and probably without conscious contemplation, meant, to him and researchers at the time, a male warrior.

Viking Burials— Cremations and Inhumations

The Viking Age society had burial practices that included cremations of various kinds as well as a number of different types of *inhumation* burials, in which the body is left whole and put in the ground. Some of these differences relate to regional traditions, while others are attributed to specific contexts (like the chamber graves). High-status burials were present in all forms of burial practice.

Graves were often covered by earth mounds. The size of the earth mound that was constructed over the grave was also significant. Graves covered by great mounds and/or large stones signaled burials of chieftains or other high-ranking individuals (both men and women). These are most often cremations. They could include horses and other animals that were placed on the pyre, as well as extensive grave goods, much like in the chamber burials.

Inhumation burial practice was less common, as were boat graves, which could be either inhumations or cremations and always represent people of higher social status.

Many people didn't get a grave at all—their bodies were either disposed of in water or their ashes scattered without a formal burial. However, we don't know who those people were or whether their status was involved. Cremation in itself doesn't mean low status—plenty of high-status folk were burned. If anything, the differences seem to be regional.

IT ALL ADDED UP

The full collection of weapons, the two horses, the strategy game, the foreign clothing and adornment, the positioning of the grave, the location of the grave, the positioning of the body, the type of grave, the sealing of the grave—these were all indicators of the burial of a significant individual. Stolpe knew it. He was well aware he had uncovered a remarkable example of an important Viking warrior. In fact, he pronounced Bj 581 to be "perhaps the most remarkable grave of all the graves in this field."

And because in Stolpe's time the belief was that all Viking warriors were men, his field notes described Bj 581 as the grave of a high-ranking male warrior.

One of Stolpe's greatest accomplishments was his detailed documentation. He stated what he saw. It was all new to him. Archaeologists who came after Stolpe were able to use his documentation to answer questions that he could not have conceived.

With the passage of time, the viewpoints on the Birka finds evolved and science advanced. One of the advancements was the science of **osteology**, the study of bones, which raised a question about the person's "maleness."

4

BIRKA TODAY

BIRKA IS UNDISPUTED as a significant Viking trading center. Its town site of approximately thirteen acres once swarmed with life. Ships sailed in and out of its multiple harbors.

The bustling Viking market town, where manufacturing and trade occurred, was located at the north end of the island in an area called the Black Earth. It was so named because its surface has an eight-foot depth of rich soil brimming with evidence of intense human activity.

Close to the Black Earth, on a low but commanding hill, stands an oval-shaped fort, protected on the inland side by a defensive wall of earth and stones called a *rampart*. Birka's rampart had at least three gateways, likely to accommodate entrance from the various harbors. On the sea side, it was protected by one-hundred-foot cliffs.

The houses found in this area were constructed using vertical wooden posts to hold up walls and bear the weight of the roofs and wooded planks called *staves*. Excavator Holger Arbman called the structures that were constructed of big vertical baulks of timber, clay, and moss *blockhouses*. Some buildings were living spaces, and others were shops for manufacturing and marketing. It is believed that the king lived on the nearby island of Adelsö in an estate called Hovgården, but there was also a large manor-type home on Birka's Korshamn Bay.

Birka's craftspeople produced and traded jewelry, textiles, weapons, furs, iron goods, and other valuables. Birka traders acquired furs of species including bear, otter, beaver, fox, and marten. These were sourced from the Sámi people of the north, as well as people from northern Russia and Finland. Traders from far and wide met in Birka and exchanged their items for Birka's products, which were some of the finest goods in the world at the time. When they left, they took Birka goods to far-flung locales. Similarly, Birka traders took local goods on their travels and brought back precious items.

One of the ways archaeologists know what was traded is by examining the artifacts in graves. The graves held many objects that Vikings created and traded for, including glass and metal objects; pottery from what is now Germany; clothing and textiles made of silk from China, Persia, and the **Byzantine Empire**; and Byzantine brocade cloth embroidered with fine gold thread, and beautifully coiled cords. Other items exchanged included amber, honey, reindeer antlers, hand-carved antler horn combs, and walrus tusks.

Ceramic jug from a grave in Birka.
National Historical Museum,
Swedish History Museum/SHM
(CC BY), Wikimedia Commons

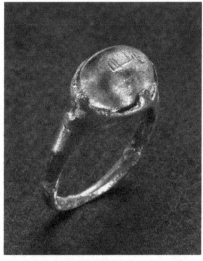

Caliphate ring found in a Birka grave.
National Historical Museum,
Swedish History Museum/SHM
(CC BY), Wikimedia Commons

Rider-shaped silver dress fitting, found in a chamber grave in Hemlanden, below the city wall of Birka. *Photo: Christer Åhlin. National Historical Museum, Swedish History Museum/SHM (CC BY), Wikimedia Commons*

Silver buckle found in Birka grave Bj 750. The prong, which was probably made of iron, is missing. *Photo: Jens Mohr. National Historical Museum, Swedish History Museum/SHM (CC BY)*

Coins found in a Birka grave.
National Historical Museum, Swedish History Museum/SHM (CC BY)

Coins found on the site were traced to northern Germany and the Caliphate, a territory ruled during the first and second century by a Muslim emperor called a *caliph* that included the Middle East and North Africa.

Any incoming ships had to traverse thirty miles of islands east of Stockholm and eighteen miles farther through island-spotted Lake Mälar. It is hard to imagine that this quiet, grassy, birch-studded island was such a hub of traffic. Yet, as Birka was a town full of valuable goods, security must have been on the minds of the people who founded it. A line of offshore wood pilings protected the main harbor. The rampart wall around the town center was seven to twelve meters wide and at least two meters high. Openings in the fence may have had high towers.

All of this required Birka to have a large contingent of protectors and fighters. Pretty much any warrior who wanted a job could find one in Birka. According to archaeologist and Birka expert Charlotte Hedenstierna-Jonson:

> Fortifications on land and in the water were constructed along with the town and then further strengthened and enhanced as the trading network expanded. In the early tenth century a permanent garrison of troops was placed directly outside the fort, overlooking the town and the harbour (Hedenstierna-Jonson 2016). The garrison consisted of a number of houses of different functions, including a smithy and storage houses, within an area enclosed by ramparts and wooden constructions. The most extensive feature was a great hall, approximately 200 m², with slightly bow-sided walls and short end facing the waterfront. Within, the large open space held the remains of a high seat and two long hearths, as would be expected in a hall. But in this particular case it was also a house made of weapons, as hundreds of knives had been incorporated into the fabric of the structure. In addition, stored in wooden chests and hanging along the walls were spears, arrows, and shields. The building was at last the actual scene of a battle, with traces of fighting and fragments of more weapons scattered throughout the interior, before the hall was destroyed by fire.

With this volume of *martial* (wartime) activity, it was not unexpected that Birka should have its need for a martial leadership structure and people with higher-order strategic skills to advise and contribute to decision-making. And when it came to burying warriors at Birka, the ranks dictated varying types of graves.

Much of what we know about Birka's history comes from a book titled *The Life of St. Anskar*, about a missionary who traveled to Birka with the objective of converting Vikings to Catholicism. It was written by his pupil, Rimbert, around the year 875 CE. Anskar made two journeys to Birka, one in approximately 830 CE and the second in approximately 850 CE. Rimbert described the journey and arrival in the town:

> With great difficulty they accomplished their long journey on foot, traversing also the intervening seas, where it was possible, by ship, and eventually arriving at the Swedish port called Birka. They were kindly received here by the king, who was called Björn, whose messengers had informed him of the reason for which they had come. When he understood the object of their mission, and had discussed the matter with his friends, with the approval and consent of all, he granted them to remain there and to preach the gospel of Christ, and offered liberty to any who desired to accept their teaching.

Rimbert tells of an attack on Birka while Anskar was there when the citizens and traders sheltered in a fortification, the remains of which are believed to be the garrison. From the fort's summit it was possible to see great distances along the waterways that led to the island.

The Law of Birka, *Björköarätt,* reveals that Birka may have already had a code of law as early as the ninth century. There was also a king who had complete control, but even he could not easily change the law, which evolved from age-old word-of-mouth tradition among inhabitants. Birka was located between three different local courts, called *Things,* and at the borders of two

Monument to Anskar still standing in Birka.
Photo: Udo Schröter. Wikimedia Commons

separate districts, called *folklands*. This may have made the rules a bit confusing.

The king, like most kings, had an excellent arrangement. He could purchase newly imported goods before of everyone else, so he effectively controlled the quantity of goods in the market and the price.

Birka was abandoned in the 970s CE. The growth of the town of Sigtuna around the same time leads many to presume Birka residents found a new home there. It has been speculated that they may have left due to shifting water levels and routes and/or because the larger ships couldn't fit in the waterways.

Today, visitors can see the numerous burial mounds on the island at Birka. They present a rolling, grassy surface.

Birka grave mounds.
Nils Lagergren / Kulturmiljöbild, Riksantikvarieämbetet, Wikimedia Commons

In 1993 Birka was made a UNESCO World Heritage Site, which is an area with legal protection under an international treaty administered by the United Nations. To be selected, a site must have cultural or natural heritage value to humanity.

Birka Excavation History

The first scientific excavations at Birka were begun in the early nineteenth century and have continued ever since. Stolpe first dug in 1871 and was followed in the 1940s by Holger Arbman, who began publishing Stolpe's papers and results. Arbman's collection has become the major catalog of Viking Age artifacts, today housed at the Swedish History Museum in Stockholm. Arbman also conducted excavations of his own on the town rampart and was followed by a long list of other experts who worked at the site:

- 1932, Holger Arbman: The town rampart
- 1934, Holger Arbman and Greta Arwidsson: The garrison
- 1969–1971, Björn Ambrosiani and Birgit Arrhenius: Jetties in the settlement area
- 1975–1981, Birgit Arrhenius, Greta Arwidsson, and Lena Holmquist: Cemeteries Ormknös and Kärrbacka
- 1987–1989, Lena Holmquist: Town rampart and terraces by the rampart
- 1990–1995, Björn Ambrosiani: Parts of the settlement with a town plot, including workshops and other buildings
- 1995–2004, Lena Holmquist: The fortifications (the hillfort and garrison)
- 1997–2016, Charlotte Hedenstierna-Jonson: Codirector for some seasons in 1997–2004 and a general member for the remainder
- 2010–2014, marine archaeologists led by Andreas Olsson: Underwater and land excavations in the harbor zone
- 2014–2016, Sven Kalmring and Lena Holmquist: The land-based part of the harbor zone
- 2019–2020, Sven Kalmring, Lena Holmquist, and Sven Isaksson: The town rampart

Birka experts, plus a host of other archaeologists, have led expeditions, researched, studied, and continue to study the Birka site, specializing in coins, fabrics, jewelry, weapons, forms of burial, and more. The wealth of grave goods recovered in Birka is considered unparalleled in any other Viking settlement. Their studies have provided tremendous insight into the pivotal trading town and added to global knowledge about the Viking Age.

5

A CLOSER LOOK AT VIKING BONES BY OSTEOLOGISTS AND ARCHAEOLOGISTS

OSTEOLOGY, THE STUDY OF BONES, is generally used in one of three ways. The first way is to assist in the identification of dead bodies. Under these circumstances, osteologists are working with pathologists, the medical doctors who document the cause of death. Osteological assessments can become evidence in an insurance or criminal case file. Osteologists may even testify in court. These days, with trials being broadcast, that means they might be on TV.

A second way osteology is used is to study dinosaur bones. Under these circumstances osteologists are working with paleontologists, who are most known for excavating dinosaur bones.

Yet a third way osteology is used is the evaluation of bones from archaeological digs. Even though osteology has been around for a while, in the mid-1900s osteologists began providing archaeologists with inventories of the bones found in both ancient graves and **funeral pyres**. Such inventories were used to compile tables for the archaeologists to consult in the assessments of their digs. From these tables they could perform comparative analysis that advanced their research.

Being an osteologist involved with archaeological research is like being a detective. It requires an understanding of:

- anatomy and skeletal structure;
- disease and trauma to bones;
- mineral effect on bones;
- biology and isotopes (which can indicate what people ate or where they lived);
- the effect of the grave structure itself;
- grave goods (things that were buried with the person);
- **funereal** practices (everything from cremation to sacrifice to burial with jeweled garments);
- population migration patterns; and
- so much more.

The human adult skeleton has approximately 206 bones and thirty-two permanent teeth. Bones grow quickly in early life, and disease and trauma can leave their mark on them. They are also sensitive to a variety of environmental issues affecting form and composition. Ancient bones may be thickened, thinned, bowed, perforated, or altered in ways that are informative about quality of life, lifestyle, and behavior.

WHAT OSTEOLOGISTS DO

Osteologists use morphology, bone chemistry, and context to assess ancient bones.

Morphology

Morphology means looking at the bones and examining their form, comparing them to the same bones in other skeletons, and comparing them to bones in the same skeleton in order to determine their variation and function. They are also examined for similarities and differences across populations. Morphology can help in evaluating even fragments of bones and can be used to model the missing parts or pieces, giving osteologists a realistic picture of the full bone. Morphological examination includes the extensive use of both still cameras and video for the documentation of images and for modeling. Computer-generated models can be created and examined from all angles.

Bone Chemistry

Bone chemistry can tell scientists something about the person's age when they died, their diet, where they lived or visited, or diseases or medical conditions they may have had. Bone chemistry came into use by osteologists and other scientists in the archaeological field in the late 1970s and has proved to be a boon for archaeology.

The element carbon takes a lead role in this area. Carbon, like the earth's various elements, is made up of atoms. Carbon particles exist in the atmosphere in three forms: 99 percent is carbon-12 (^{12}C), and the rest is made up of carbon-13 (^{13}C) and carbon-14 (^{14}C). These are also called *carbon isotopes*.

When carbon atoms in the atmosphere come into contact with oxygen, they form carbon dioxide. Plants then absorb the carbon dioxide into their fibers through a process called *photosynthesis*. People and animals eat the plants, and thus, the carbon atoms are inside them. The carbon atoms remain in the people or plants after they die, except there is a difference: ^{12}C and ^{13}C don't change in amount after death but ^{14}C does. Carbon-14 (also known as radio-carbon) dissipates. For this reason, it is called an *unstable isotope*. This instability or dissipation is what makes it useful in estimating age of a sample.

Estimating Age or Carbon 14 (^{14}C) Dating

The decay of ^{14}C can be measured with reasonable accuracy (plus or minus twenty years) back to approximately sixty thousand years ago. When a person is alive, the ratio of ^{14}C to ^{12}C atoms is nearly constant. ^{14}C atoms are always decaying, but they are constantly being replaced, and the ratio is being maintained. But after an organism dies, ^{14}C is not replaced as it decays. The rate of this decay is stated in the form of a half-life of fifty-seven hundred years (plus or minus thirty years). This means that after fifty-seven hundred years, only half the ^{14}C will be left. So, for example, if the skeleton of a warrior is unearthed, and in testing, researchers determine that half the ^{14}C in the warrior's bones has decayed away (to put it another way, that the ratio of ^{14}C to ^{12}C is half of the ratio of ^{14}C to ^{12}C for things living today), the team can estimate that the warrior died fifty-seven hundred years ago.

Reliability

Recent research has questioned the reliability of radiocarbon dating. According to archaeologist Sturt W. Manning and his team, who examined tree rings of the same period in different hemispheres, the standard calibration tables that show the decay rate of ^{14}C have assumed the radiocarbon levels to be the same across hemispheres, and that is not the case. Evidence showed that the average difference in radiocarbon ages of samples across hemispheres was nineteen years, meaning ^{14}C decayed slightly faster or slower in different geographic locations. Manning, a professor at Cornell University, urged a round of revisions to the calibrated tables and a reset of the thinking on this variable. The recalibration began in 2020, and while the expectation is that the changes will be subtle, they are still expected to be of key importance to redating important archaeological finds.

In addition, carbon dating may not be as reliable after 1940. Anything that died since that time will be affected to some degree by the existence of nuclear reactors and open-air nuclear tests, which can add more ^{14}C to material that is being tested, making it more difficult to date it.

Diet, Travels, Diseases, or Medical Conditions

The chemicals that remain in bones don't have to have carbon-14's built-in decay timer to be useful to researchers. Unlike ^{14}C, the ratio of ^{12}C to ^{13}C in the atmosphere never changes. There are always one hundred ^{12}C atoms to one ^{13}C atom. And ^{13}C is a stable isotope, meaning that it doesn't decay away over time. This stability is useful in identifying what a person ate, where they traveled (because the food might be different in another location), and any medical condition or diseases they may have had.

During photosynthesis, plants absorb the carbon atoms in the air, water, and soil into their tissues, but the chemical ratio gets altered uniquely by the plants due to climate and regions (sun, water, woodlands, wetlands). As humans and animals eat the plants, and it turns into their hair, teeth, and bones, this unique local ratio remains the same. So, if you know the ratio of ^{12}C to ^{13}C in the bones of a human or animal, you have clues as to where the plants they ate were grown and consumed.

Researchers use elements other than carbon to learn about the lives of ancient humans and animals. They also look at oxygen, nitrogen, strontium, hydrogen, sulfur, lead, and others.

South African archaeologist Nikolaas van der Merwe performed the first stable isotope research in archaeology in the 1970s. He excavated at the African Iron Age site of Kgopolwe 3 in the Transvaal Lowveld of South Africa, called Phalaborwa, and uncovered something very remarkable through chemical study of bones.

> Van der Merwe found a human male skeleton in an ash heap that did not look like the other burials from the village. The skeleton was different, morphologically, from the other inhabitants of Phalaborwa, and he had been buried in a completely different manner than the typical villager. The man looked like a Khoisan; and Khoisans should not have been at Phalaborwa, who were ancestral Sotho tribesmen. Van der Merwe and his colleagues J. C. Vogel and Philip Rightmire decided to look at the chemical signature in his bones, and the initial results suggested that the man was a sorghum farmer from a Khoisan village who somehow had died at Kgopolwe 3.

Since 1977, applications of stable **isotope analysis** have increased in number and breadth. They have been used to investigate the diets of our ancient ancestors to determine if they were immigrants or had been born locally. In criminal investigations, isotopes have also been used to arrest ivory and rhino horn poachers by tracing the origin of the tusks and horns, and to break up smuggling rings by revealing the agricultural source of cocaine and heroin. They have even traced the cotton fiber in counterfeit money.

Context

Depending on the project, osteologists sometimes go on location. This is where they consider grave context. The context or environment could be a burned site or an inhumation. There may be ashes, partial bones, and unburned bones. If there is a grave, it may have unique structural qualities. It may be simple or ornate. There may be one skeleton or more than one skeleton. With the skeleton(s) there may be grave goods including personal items such as clothing, jewelry, weapons, weights and measures, pots, or vessels. And the very location of the grave and its surroundings may have significance.

Thus, using morphology, chemistry, and context, osteologists can tell a great deal about bones. If certain characteristics of bone material are sufficiently preserved, they can identify whether, in a group of varied bones, they are human or animal. They can also determine whether they are all from the same skeleton or from different skeletons. Additionally, it is possible to identify if they suffered bone-specific illness, injury, or environmental impact, as well as what the person ate, if they traveled, whether they are biologically male or female, and how old they are.

ANATOMY THAT MATTERS IN DETERMINING SEX IN ANCIENT BONES

While there is a great deal of overlap in shape and size of male and female bones, some bones are distinctly male or female, making it possible to estimate a skeleton's sex using just those bones.

Bones can be divided into three categories: the flat bones, which include the pelvis, shoulder blades, ribs, breastbone, and skull; the tubular bones, which include the short and long bones of the arms, legs, hands, and feet; and the irregular bones, which include the kneecaps, vertebrae, wrists, and ankles.

While there are certain general shapes of bones in male and female skeletons that are similar, morphologic examination reveals many differences:

- *The skull*: In general, the male skull is larger and heavier. For example, the muscular ridges are larger, the occipital protuberance (raised area at the base of the skull), is more developed, the teeth are larger, and it is less rounded than the female skull.
- *The spine*: In general, the male spine is larger. For example, the lumbar region is greater, the total length is greater, the sacrum is longer, and the **auricular surface** extends to the third vertebra, whereas in a female it extends to the second vertebra. Also, the auricular surface in females is raised and in males is flat.
- *The sternum*: The male sternum is in general at least twice as long as the female sternum.
- *The clavicle*: The male clavicle is an average of 0.39 inches (10 mm) longer than the female.
- *The pelvis*: The pelvis shows the most significant and reliable difference between males and females. It is cited as 90 to 95 percent accurate in determining sex. The characteristics can be identified by visual examination and by measuring. The female pelvis is specially adapted to giving birth. The obturator foramina are

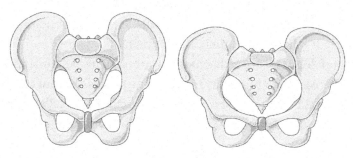

Male pelvis: anterior view   Female pelvis: anterior view

Illustration comparing male and female pelvis.
Servier Medical Art, Wikimedia Commons

more triangular in females and oval in males. This and other aspects of the female pelvis lend it to being large enough to allow the head of a baby to pass through.

- *The long bones:* In males the long bones are in general longer and larger, the head of a bone is larger, and the shaft is broader and thicker. Except for size, these differences can be vague. However, they have proved to be helpful even in the case of poorly preserved and fragmented bones.

ARCHAEOLOGISTS, ANTHROPOLOGISTS, AND HISTORIANS

The first people to dig up ancient remains and rummage about in old graves were basically treasure hunters and collectors of antiquities. By the late nineteenth century, these pilferers were replaced with early professionals and scholars who were interested in studying the development of human civilization and cultures. Eventually, their study led to scholarship, and the field of archaeology emerged.

Archaeologists have been portrayed as romantic action heroes, like Indiana Jones, or dust-covered professors with netted helmets digging up stone tablets by the pyramids. In reality, the activity of early archaeologists has evolved into an academic discipline with ethical codes.

Archaeologists are concerned with **material culture**, the things people have left behind. This can include tools, weapons, jewelry, clothing, structures, art, writings, pots, food remains, animal remains, plant remains, and their own remains.

Anthropologists and archaeologists are similar but different. Anthropologists study humanity, in its broadest sense, through culture. So, it is said (in the United States) that archaeology falls under the umbrella description of anthropology. Archaeologists and anthropologists work toward many of the same goals and sometimes do it in the same way. But archaeologists will also explain that they link their excavated objects to human behavior and use their data far differently than anthropologists.

Historians and archaeologists also have overlapping interests. Historians and archaeologists both study the human past. Historians focus on documentary sources—primarily written records but also maps, texts, runestones, ancient inscriptions, and other such items. Archaeologists technically draw on all remains. So when they consider documentary sources, they are historians also.

Differences do exist, however, in the way archaeologists study history. Archaeology involves excavating, recording, and preserving. But this is really only the day-to-day part of the job. There is more to it: the theory part. Everything that is recovered needs to be analyzed and interpreted. Archaeologists work like detectives trying to develop a picture of life in an ancient time. It requires assembling a complicated collection of clues into an interpretation of the scene.

All the remains found in a site are considered archaeological data. This could include a ruined building, a grave, pots, textiles, jewelry, bones, and weapons—things that resulted from human activity. Archaeological data is always undergoing change, even from its creation. For example, the human body decays, buildings are burned or destroyed by weather, or years later other humans interact with the items and change them. It's a constant process of transformation, both natural and intentional. All the remains, in their transformational state, that are taken from or recorded at the site, are considered the archaeological record. These things can be easily destroyed even under the best preservation conditions, but the archaeological record is considered the basis of all research.

Every archaeologist is responsible for preparing accurate records of the things they find. This could be a list of artifacts (items like pots and brooches), drawings of excavated graves, or drawings or photographs of uncovered buildings or landscape constructions. They use hand drawings, photographs, aerial surveys, and any means of other technology used to accurately examine a site.

One of the most difficult tasks for an archaeologist is to know how to interpret ancient remains, particularly when they have gone through some form of transformation. The prime aim is to uncover the most accurate picture of the original scene. The methods for going about this vary. It depends on whether the site has never been interpreted before or whether this will be a reinterpretation. In the case of first interpretation, the process includes a deep dive into all research on the subject, then developing a theory, if one is warranted. In the case of a reinterpretation, the process includes an evaluation of the interpretation(s) of the previous archaeologist(s) and a determination as to how much of it the new archaeologist agrees with or doesn't and why.

An archaeologist has a professional responsibility to publish articles and books about his or her research and to respond to the research of others. The publication should state the objective of the research (the hypothesis), the data used to test it, and the interpretation of the results.

Archaeologists are people with boundless enthusiasm, patience, a love of detail, good organizational skills, cultural sensitivity, ethics, a sense of humor, and a graduate degree (a master's degree and/or PhD). It can be dirty and buggy when they excavate in the field. There will be lab work, research, writing, speaking, and lecturing. Careers can be in academia teaching and researching, in museums, and in the private sector. Some archaeologists pursue careers in the field; others stay at their desks writing about artifacts. Almost endless subareas exist in which to specialize, including osteology, cultures, geographic locations, underwater sites, fires, caves, burials, weapons, women, and on and on.

One thing is certain: archaeologists experience a lot of the world that the rest of us never get to see. They have a very special perspective on us humans.

6

OSTEOLOGISTS WEIGH IN ON THE BIRKA WARRIOR

Over one hundred years after Stolpe, osteologist Anna Kjellström examined the bones of the person in grave Bj 581. But unlike Stolpe, she didn't assume anything about the sex of the person buried in Bj 581. She examined it morphologically. When she was done, she believed the skeleton was . . . female! Arriving at this conclusion was a long path for Kjellström.

DR. ANNA KJELLSTRÖM, OSTEOLOGIST

When Anna Kjellström was young, she hung out with friends, shot free throws on the basketball court, and practiced Mozart on the flute. That is, until she was given a book about the Black Death, the horrendous plague of the Middle Ages. Something gripped her in the tale of a disease that could rage though a population and kill millions of people. She read that book over and over.

When she was studying archaeology at Uppsala University, she and other students were observing a cathedral restoration when workers unexpectedly uncovered bones. Anna was drawn to the scene and wanted to see more, do more, and be more closely involved in finding out everything about those bones. To her they

Anna Kjellström. *Photo courtesy of Niklas Björling*

were people. They once walked around, laughed, and loved. And the events of their lives were written in their remains.

Kjellström earned a bachelor's degree, master's degree, and doctorate in archaeology, with a specialty in osteology. That's a lot of bones, bones, bones. She is now a director and associate professor of osteology at Stockholm University. During her years of study and practice since 1991, she has authored many chapters and articles, edited books and articles, developed courses, taught, and researched in the field of bioarchaeology. She even performed forensic assignments for the Swedish police, acting as special advisor on the skeletal remains from the seventeenth-century Swedish battleship *Kronan*, for the Kalmar Museum.

By the time the bones of Bj 581 lay before her, she had examined thousands and thousands of bones.

HOW KJELLSTRÖM DOES HER MORPHOLOGICAL EXAMINATIONS

Anna Kjellström says her examination depends on the condition of a skeleton. She's examined skeletons where she has all or most of the bones, and she has also examined only fragments. Other times the bones are charred bits. Most times they are fragments and the preservation is poor.

Kjellström begins by laying the bones on a table. If the skeleton is complete or close to complete, she places them in the order they would be on a body. If they are all or mostly there, she can do this easily. If they are fragmented, it can take hours. If bones are from a funeral pyre, she can work for weeks sorting them.

"When I have them laid out and in the best anatomical order, I select the bones that carry the most information and examine them," she explained. "I take measurements, assess age traits, stature, teeth, and so on. I take lots of pictures as I try to understand what's gone on with this person. I look for anomalies that will reveal disease, injury, repetitive use, and I decide upon chemical testing if there are funds available."

Osteologists record in spreadsheets what they see. For example, when Kjellström examines bones for a multiperson project, she opens a database for the project and enters her measurements and impressions as she goes along. It is an inventory of her scientific observations. From these data entries in tables, she could compare individuals, and identify trends across populations.

In 2009, Kjellström created the People in Transition project. She sought insight into a particular population's cultural behavior (such as religious rituals), plagues and diseases, or wars and battle scars. She planned to examine graves from three locations: Sigtuna, the earliest Swedish town; the nearby rural Mälaren Valley; and Birka, a close island trading town. These areas overlap geographically, and the time period selected for each was similar. At least in theory, some of the individuals she would study could have actually met during their lifetimes. Certainly, it made for good comparisons.

Kjellström was the first osteologist to examine the entire Birka collection in more than three decades. Many of the graves were poorly preserved, resulting from soil pressure, soil drainage, and other factors. Additionally, it did not help that the collection had been moved and repackaged over the years.

Why would a museum's grave collections be moved? In the case of the Swedish History Museum, curators relocated the collection in anticipation of the completion of a new museum. Also, during wartime, they transferred precious artifacts to the museum's basement to protect them. The individual grave contents were also repackaged several times at the museum, from less preservative containers to more protective containers. They went from drawers to plastic bags, from plastic bags to boxes, and so on, as the technology improved.

Unfortunately, some remains were mixed up during these transfers. For example, one grave was registered as having a single person, but the container had the bones of more than one person. Kjellström considered some of these graves questionable and rejected them from the study of individual graves. She didn't ignore them entirely, though. They were considered still representative of the population and were of great interest in the larger analysis of the community.

Fortunately, some of the graves had bone material that was consistent with Stolpe's descriptions and drawings. Kjellström was able to identify a group of 236 individual graves with sufficient bone material to examine. Within the 236, some were better preserved than others. Bj 581 was one of the better ones. It was considered in good condition.

The Bj 581 box had minimal impact from the many moves and was one of the most intact collections of grave contents. However, one curiosity was that its cranium had been removed. A second oddity was that a single femur with the marking "Bj 854" had found its way into the box, sometime after the 1940s and Holger Arbman's time. Kjellström noted: "I registered the bone with all the others, but I commented that it deviated from the rest. Everything else in the case matched the original Stolpe drawings, inventory, notes, and journals of the grave Bj 581."

Kjellström wasn't the first osteologist to look at the Bj 581 bones or to note the stray femur in the box. In the 1970s an osteologist named Berit Vilkans examined the Bj 581 bones and also saw the

The third femur present in the storage box for grave Bj 581, clearly labeled "Bj 854," showing that it had been misplaced from a different burial.
Photo: Ola Myrin. Swedish History Museum/SHM (CC BY)

femur. Vilkans compared the bones to the Stolpe drawing and found that they were the correct ones for the grave. But when she saw the odd femur, she questioned whether there had been two bodies in the grave. When she made a sex determination, she did not consider the odd numbered femur, but based her finding on, among other things, the "fragment of left-sided female pelvis" marked for Bj 581. Some people in Swedish archaeological circles were aware of her findings, but they didn't draw attention, perhaps because of their unpublished nature, or the fact that osteology is considered observational and not conclusive as to sex, or the confusion of the stray femur, or that she was a female scientist. Or maybe all these things combined.

KJELLSTRÖM'S ASSESSMENT

Kjellström approached the Bj 581 box just as she had every other assessment, using recognized methods to estimate age and sex based on aspects of the pelvis and lower jaw, and measurements of the humerus and femur:

> I examined every bone from grave Bj 581 and found that
> not only were the human bones labeled with the grave

number, so were the horses' bones, and most of the artefacts, including the weapons and game pieces. There was
a lower jaw, a complete spine, humerus, forearms, hip
bones and lower extremities and partial feet. They shared
the same character and color on the surface.

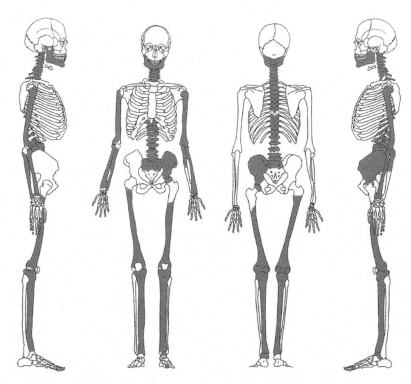

Shaded bones are the ones found in the Bj 581 grave.
Original illustrations by Buikstra & Ubelaker (1994), modified by Anna Kjellström.

I laid out the bones in the sitting order to match the
drawing. Generally, the bones were poorly preserved and
there weren't many features that I could look at."

The **epiphyseal union** was completed on all preserved
bones, and the appearance of the auricular surface of the
left hip bone met the morphological criteria for phase 3,

Bj 581 bones laid out in sitting order as they were found in the grave and to match the drawing.
Ola Myrin, Swedish History Museum/ SHM (CC BY)

which is different morphological criteria associated with age changes. The dental wear of the lower molars was clear but moderate. In all, this suggested that the individual was above 30 years of age.

Additionally, the long bones were thin, slender and *gracile* which provided further indirect support for the assessment. I observed no significant skeletal alterna-tions [changing bone patterns], although I documented degenerative changes in the form of osteophytes [bony lumps] on the ventral bodies or the thoracic vertebrae, and marginal lipping [overgrowth of bone] and sur-face pitting of the apophyseal facet joints [spine joints that allow flexibility] of the third to fifth lumbar verte-brae. Additionally, the distal part of the medial side of the diaphysis of the tibiae [bones between the knees and ankles] exhibited mild periosteal new bone formation.

I observed no pathological or traumatic injuries.

The **greater sciatic notch** of the hip was broad, and wide **preauricular sulcus** was present. This, together with the lack of a projection of the mental eminence on the man-dible, assessed the individual as female.

I concluded the skeleton was very highly likely to be female.

Why did Kjellström qualify her assessment as "very highly likely female" rather than "female"?

Osteologists often hedge their bets when they make a sex assessment because the assessments are based on human morphology—human observation—which can to some extent vary between people and which is not considered to be abso-lute. They are observations—expert, scientific observations—but in the end, only observations.

KJELLSTRÖM GOT A SECOND . . . AND A THIRD OPINION

Because this was such a famous grave that had been assumed male for over a century, and because it was good practice, Kjellström asked two other osteologists to do independent blind assessments. Without telling them what she had found or what the record reflected, she asked osteologists Petra Molnar and Elin Ahlin Sundman to assess the skeleton. They each, separately and independently, came up with the same conclusion: the person was very highly likely to be female.

Kjellström didn't set out to wake up a female Viking warrior. Nor did she intend to vindicate Berit Vilkans. She was methodically going through a group of graves that were selected for the purposes of the People in Transition project, which included an effort to identify sex. And, well, there it was. So what to do about it?

She elected not to deviate from her original purpose. The documentation went into the larger database, just as for all the skeletons, so the data could be used for various purposes. Later, when she wrote the paper for the entire project, she called it out because it was interesting . . . though she knew it would raise eyebrows.

"I knew it would be controversial since it was about a chamber grave where striking equipment consisting of, among other things, an ax, a sword, and two horses have contributed to the archaeological interpretation that it was a man. That was not my focus in the People in Transition study, but I didn't want to ignore it because it was a significant grave."

In the paper she wrote: "Another interesting (and possibly controversial) find was a grave where the preserved bones do fit the original nineteenth century drawings and descriptions. This is a chamber grave furnished with fine armor and sacrificed horses. Nevertheless, three different osteological examinations [Kjellström, Molnar, and Sundman] all found that the individual was a woman." And because ethical osteologists always explicitly draw attention to any uncertainties the evidence may have identified, she added, "Whether these are the correct bones for this grave or whether it opens up reinterpretations of weapons graves in Birka, it is too early to say."

Anna Kjellström with the Bj 581 skeleton.
Photo by Sebastian Peiter, ©2019 Urban Canyons

Kjellström says she added this to her report only because she had not yet completed the task of going through the inventory list and comparing it with the description in the archaeological record in a careful and consistent manner, but she and osteoarchaeologist and professor Jan Storå completed that later, so in fact the contents of the box matched the Stolpe record.

When Kjellström presented the results at a conference in 2011, the reaction was mixed. One person said, "Wow," and another said, "That can't be." Others came up to her after the presentation with suggestions for alternate interpretations of the grave. She found this curious since her findings as to the bones were scientific sex assessments.

For Kjellström the sex of Bj 581 was more a statistic than a social or gender implication. She had included the grave in her study because it fit the study's criteria. But the People in Transition project would not be the last Kjellström heard of Bj 581.

7

WAIT! *WHAT?* THE FAMOUS BIRKA WARRIOR REALLY *IS* FEMALE!

ARCHAEOLOGIST CHARLOTTE HEDENSTIERNA-JONSON came to Birka by way of war—she was interested in warriors. As a field archaeologist, she painstakingly excavated and researched the martial aspects of the Viking trading town. The site had so many things to examine that she eventually became an expert on Birka's warriors and their ways.

DR. CHARLOTTE HEDENSTIERNA-JONSON: THE ARCHAEOLOGIST WHO SELECTED BJ 581 FOR DNA TESTING

Born in Sweden, Charlotte grew up hearing the Norse myths and stories of the Viking people who lived during the period of 750 CE to 1050 CE. In school she learned that the farming and seafaring people who lived in the Viking town of Birka developed a center of craft and trade. She also learned the Viking warriors had a notorious and brutal reputation for raiding and plundering.

Her family vacations included sailing to Birka and picnicking on its grassy hills. She might have let herself imagine a dragon-headed Viking longship being loaded for a trading voyage—goats bleating, children clinging to mothers who were saying goodbye to men who

Charlotte Hedenstierna-Jonson. *Photo courtesy of Charlotte Hedenstierna-Jonson*

would be gone for months—or longships with snakeheads where warriors mustered, huffed, and jostled their shields and weapons as they boarded for raiding adventures. She could hear the bustle of trade in the town, the sizzle of the blacksmith fire, the clank of the hammer forging a sword. She knew there were thousands of Viking graves on the island and that they told the story of a people of commerce but also a people of extreme violence. This intrigued her. She wanted to know how and why they did this. Thus, it was no surprise that when she grew up she wanted to study these people and their warring tendencies.

Hedenstierna-Jonson earned a bachelor's and a master's in art history, and a master's degree and a doctorate in archaeology. She's also done quite a bit of fieldwork—much of it in Birka on the Martial Project, a multiyear excavation project carried out at Birka that was led by Lena Holmquist-Olausson. Now Hedenstierna-Jonson is considered a leading expert on Birka—perhaps *the* expert on Bj 581.

"I think it is important to acknowledge that what we as researchers are aiming to do is to understand people and societies that actually existed, with all the complexities that this implies. It is my firm conviction that the interpretive process, relying on both material and theoretic framework, should be characterized by transparency and consistency, making it possible to trace the steps from interpretation back to archaeological evidence."

—Charlotte Hedenstierna-Jonson

When she started in the early 2000s, there weren't many female archaeologists. She didn't have an easy time. She remembers a dirty, muddy field at Birka where the sun beat down, warming a chilly Swedish afternoon. She recalled, "We all squatted and troweled through layers of black dirt and an older male archaeologist paused near me and said, 'Now why would a young woman want to study war and violence?'"

It wasn't as if she was the only woman researching Viking war and warriors at the site. The leader of the excavation was a woman, Lena Holmquist, who also headed the research project linked to the excavation. Lena would later become Hedenstierna-Jonson's PhD supervisor.

And there were others. "We called each other 'trench mates' and 'mining horses,' and the group included archaeologists named Laila, Helena, Lotta, Sara, and Cecilia. During both my master's and PhD programs I also had several female advisors. And in fact, there is a long line of female archaeology scholars—all the way back to the time of Hjalmar Stolpe."

Charlotte Hedenstierna-Jonson and some of her trench mates in the field.
Photo courtesy of Charlotte Hedenstierna-Jonson

Hedenstierna-Jonson had a pretty tough skin when it came to the male heckling. "Like most professional women do, I dusted off my hands and I shrugged him off. I was confident in what I was doing. I relished the mud, the bugs, the weather, the backbreaking work—I was excited when I uncovered traces of the lives of fierce ancient people. I guess I was 'showing the front of my feet,' and he reacted to it."

In the United States, a girl may not have heard the expression "showing the front of your feet," but in Sweden it has a special meaning, according to Hedenstierna-Jonson: "It refers to a person—particularly a woman—who becomes visible or notable in their profession, and who thus draws heightened scrutiny. So, my knees may have been smudged with dirt, but my outlook was optimistic. I retained my curiosity about people. I still wanted to know where they lived and how they interacted with each other. I still had a longtime interest in their art and art objects. I still believe that art often asks the question: *What does it mean to be human*? He didn't bully me off of anything."

Groundbreaking Women of Swedish Archaeology

Women have a significant history in Swedish archaeology.

Hanna Rydh (1891–1964) graduated in literature, history, and archaeology, and at Uppsala University in 1919, she was the first woman in Sweden to receive a PhD in archaeology. She conducted archaeological excavations at Adelsö and in the province of Gästrikland. Rydh was offered a research grant in 1922, when she had a young son, and someone questioned her availability. She notoriously replied, "My son's birth makes no difference!"

Greta Arwidsson (1906–1998) obtained a master of philosophy degree in 1930 with emphasis in Latin, geography, and history. She worked on the Valsgärde excavations and received a PhD on the boat graves unearthed there. Arwidsson later became the head archaeologist for Gotland, and then became professor of archaeology at Stockholm University.

Birgit Arrhenius (1932–) is a professor at Stockholm University. She founded and was the first head of the Archaeology Research Laboratory in 1976. She participated in excavations in Helgö and Birka. In 1992, using laser scanning, she demonstrated that a dancing warrior, who appeared on one of the cast bronze Torslunda plates that were used to make helmet decorations, had one eye stricken out, indicating the image of the one-eyed god Odin.

Hedenstierna-Jonson continued to avidly pursue her study of Birka, the well-fortified, wealthy center of crafts and trade. Traders came into Birka with raw materials and goods from the coastline of

Charlotte Hedenstierna-Jonson at work in the Swedish History Museum.
Photo: Linda Wåhlander. Swedish History Museum/SHM (CC BY)

the Baltic and beyond, and Birka's workshops took the raw materials and turned them into the jewelry, textiles, and other valuables that, together with slaves, were traded for silver and other items. Of course, warriors were needed to protect the town's riches from raids. As such, a permanent garrison of troops was posted outside the fort and stood constant vigil over the town and the harbor.

Warriors were also needed to do the distance trading. They launched ventures into today's Russia and Ukraine and through the Baltic region as far as the Byzantine metropolis of Constantinople and the Eurasian Steppe. Sometimes, Viking ships had both raiders and traders aboard. It was also possible for a trading run to turn sour and end in plundering. Then again, there were times of straight up raiding and plundering.

THE ATLAS PROJECT

Hedenstierna-Jonson soon became a curator at the Swedish History Museum, with special responsibility for the late Iron Age. The late Iron Age, 400–1050 CE, includes the Viking Age. At approximately the same time, she was invited to join the Atlas of 1000 Ancient Genomes Project ("The Atlas Project") as the Iron Age specialist. In this role she would lead the Iron Age archaeogenetic study.

The Atlas Project is a massive effort to research Swedish DNA. Multiple universities and multidisciplinary researchers are creating a catalog of ancient Swedish **human genomes** (DNA) through osteology and specialized testing. Experts from fields including genetics, history, osteology, archaeology, and more have gathered

Maja Krzewinska, geneticist.
Photo courtesy of Niklas Björling

Torun Zachrisson, archaeologist.
Photo courtesy of Niklas Björling

for this project. Thousands of skeletons have been selected.

Hedenstierna-Jonson worked closely with Anna Kjellström, who had also joined the project, archaeologist Torun Zachrisson, and geneticist Maja Krzewińska. Together, they selected the skeletons from across Sweden to be DNA tested.

"Of course, we wanted to sample as many skeletons as possible, from as many contexts as possible. Without hesitation, I put Bj 581 on the list," Hedenstierna-Jonson recalled. "I knew the genomic testing would provide a wealth of information about it, not the least of which would be the individual's sex. It was an easy pick for a lot of reasons: it was a significant grave based upon Stolpe's classification as a high-ranking male warrior, and Kjellström and other osteologists had assessed it as female, throwing the issue of the sex into question."

"Anna, Torun, and I had our heads in our paperwork when Maja appeared at our open office door. Her face was calm. She simply said without excitement, 'Bj 581 is XX chromosome.' I know Anna was pleased to have her assessment confirmed. I wasn't all

Office mates at the Atlas Project: Torun Zachrisson, Anna Kjellström, Maja Krzewińska, and Charlotte Hedenstierna-Jonson.
Photo courtesy of Niklas Björling

that surprised since I trusted Anna. She'd done her work. She'd had two other osteologists do blind tests of the same samples, and they had come up with the same result. The skeleton was female. Maja had just delivered the news that validated Anna's conclusions."

It was still big news. The full Atlas team headed to what they called the "war room" for a briefing from the geneticists. Everyone was getting a chance to pepper them with questions about the results. They would hear not only about the sex but also the DNA testing results.

The lab used was the Archaeological Research Laboratory (ARL) at Stockholm University.

ARL is a DNA testing facility designed solely to analyze ancient DNA from archaeological materials from all ages. The uniqueness of ARL is the combination of archaeology and science. It's a custom process. The archaeologist submits material to be tested and questions, and then the lab performs testing to address the objectives. It is premier by virtue of its chemical, biological, physical, and geological analytical methods.

The assembled Atlas team had so many questions. For several days they mulled over the sex determination and its meaning. *Could it be interpreted this way . . . ?*, *Could it be interpreted that way . . . ?*, and *What does it mean that . . . ?*

They challenged themselves to explore archaeological issues such as:

- Did we agree with the scholars who had been writing on Bj 581?
- What aspects of the material culture made it so?
- Were we satisfied that the grave was intact after the blasting of the covering rock?
- Did the skeleton in the container correctly match Stolpe's drawing and notebooks?
- What could or couldn't be implied about the gender of the person and how she or they appeared to the community?

They were interested in everything they could learn about this individual. They talked about health issues, family relations, and social relations. One person—even one who was over a thousand years old—couldn't answer all the questions they had about the people living in Birka, or all the Vikings, or all people who lived during the Iron Age, but the researchers didn't expect that. They were analyzing hundreds of Viking Age skeletons, and they expected this person would add facts to a greater context.

DID THE TEAM THINK THE DNA RESULT CHANGED HISTORY?

Everyone on the team realized this news would be of great interest. Their DNA result overturned a belief about Bj 581 that had been ingrained for over one hundred years. Not only was it significant that the famous Birka warrior was now proven to be female sexed, there were all the other social and cultural implications that flowed from it. It needed to be published.

But all these issues couldn't be easily discussed in one article. So, they decided to write two separate peer-reviewed articles. The first would address the simple but dramatic change of one factor: sex. The second would raise the other issues.

Peer Review

Peer review is a process used worldwide by academics of all disciplines to announce their research and have other academics comment on it. At its core, it's how the base of knowledge advances in a field—by announcement, validation, and/or criticism. It begins with the author(s) submitting a scholarly article in an accepted format that meets a research journal's requirements. The journal's editorial board then considers the paper for relevance to the journal and may ask reviewers to read the paper and comment.

Most peer-review journals subscribe to similar evaluation criteria. First, they expect the submitted article to be orderly, to be based on common sense, and to follow their editorial guidelines. This includes a clear title and a good abstract, or article summary. Second, they consider the interest the article will generate in a specific field and its relationship to relevant topics. It must have an up-to-date bibliography and correct description of the state of the situation and identify potential links to related discussions. Last, it must have logical soundness. In other words, has the premise been proved? Do the conclusions correspond to the data and empirical evidence?

If the article meets these criteria, it is sent out to other scholars working in the field to comment on it. The reviewers are almost always anonymous, and they won't know the identities of the authors until the paper is published. The authors never find out who reviewed their work, unless a person chooses to waive anonymity. This is the peer-review portion of the process. Often, the reviewers' comments will lead to revision of the article on matters such as clarity or phrasing. Once the revision process has been completed, the article is considered to have passed external review. At this point the journal's editorial board once again scrutinizes the final article, and if it is satisfied it measures up to its standards, the journal will publish the paper. Once it is out in the world, other academics may then submit papers of their own commenting on, supporting, or rebutting the contents of the article.

Archaeology and anthropology are two fields that use this peer-review process all the time. Above all, it is an accepted professional form of conversation between academic authors/ researchers, reviewers, and editors in which the excellence of a discovery is tested, validated, and/or challenged.

The full team on the Bj 581 article included Charlotte Hedenstierna-Jonson, Anna Kjellström, Neil Price, Torun Zachrisson, Maja Krzewińska, Verónica Sobrado, Torsten Günther, Mattias Jakobsson, Anders Götherström, and Jan Storå.

Hedenstierna-Jonson took the lead on the first paper, and others made contributions based on their expertise. Neil Price would take the lead on the second paper.

The abstract includes information about why the study was undertaken, the methods used, and the highlights of the results:

> Objectives: The objective of this study has been to confirm the sex and the affinity of an individual buried in a well-furnished warrior grave (Bj 581) in the Viking Age town of Birka, Sweden. Previously, based on the material and historical records, the male sex has been associated with the gender of the warrior and such was the case with Bj 581. An earlier osteological classification of the individual as female was considered controversial in a historical and archaeological context. A genomic confirmation of the biological sex of the individual was considered necessary to solve the issue.
>
> Materials and Methods: Genome-wide sequence data was generated in order to confirm the biological sex, to support skeletal integrity, and to investigate the genetic relationship of the individual to ancient individuals as well as modern-day groups. Additionally, a strontium isotope analysis was conducted to highlight the mobility [range of travel] of the individual.
>
> Results: The genomic results revealed the lack of a Y-chromosome and thus a female biological sex, and the mtDNA analyses support a single-individual origin of sampled elements. The genetic affinity is close to present-day North Europeans, and within Sweden to the southern and south-central region. Nevertheless, the Sr values are not conclusive as to whether she was of local or nonlocal origin.
>
> Discussion: The identification of a female Viking warrior provides a unique insight into the Viking society, social constructions, and exceptions to the norm in the Viking time-period. The results call for caution against

generalizations regarding social orders in past societies.

The article describes the DNA and isotope testing and their results. The conclusion is that the sole person in grave Bj 581 was above thirty years of age at the time of death, was approximately five feet, seven inches tall, was not originally from Birka but perhaps southern Sweden, and was female sexed.

SURPRISE! THE TEAM HAD A HARD TIME GETTING THE ARTICLE PUBLISHED

The team's submissions to the first two journals were disappointing. Both passed on it. One even said it didn't think it would interest its readers.

Finally, on April 11, 2017, Hedenstierna-Jonson sent the article out a third time. This time she sent it to the *American Journal of Physical Anthropology*. She pressed the UPLOAD key with continued confidence. She was sending them evidence of a female Viking warrior. The sex of the individual had been proven by science, and she and her colleagues had set forth all the evidence in the supplementary materials. Who wouldn't jump at this?

The *American Journal of Physical Anthropology* put their submission through its rigorous standards of review and ultimately, on August 23, 2017, accepted it. The article was published on September 8, 2017, along with its supplementary material.

THE REACTION TO THE ARTICLE

Then came another surprise. Imagine for a second that you've had a difficult time publishing a scientific paper that you thought made a major contribution to the field. You might have given up on the idea that it would create academic dialogue. You might even have concluded it was going to receive a big yawn.

Quite the opposite. The paper was an overnight sensation, and not just to excavation nerds. Its impact went way beyond the halls of academia. *Way beyond!*

"I woke up to a flurry of emails, texts, pings, and rings. I was shocked," said Hedenstierna-Jonson.

I called Neil Price who said, "We knew it would be interesting, but this is unbelievable! I'd forgotten we'd uploaded it. Have you read some of these comments?"

He was also astounded. It wasn't as if we'd purposely published a controversial paper and then braced ourselves for the impact. People were suggesting it was some mastery of media manipulation.

When I returned home to Stockholm, I was swamped with phone messages from reporters asking for interviews. As the lead author of the paper, it fell to me to be the public face of the discovery. Newspaper and magazine reporters, bloggers, podcasters, radio show hosts, YouTube videographers, and freelance writers all wanted to talk to me and to Anna Kjellström. Neil Price helped out fielding inquiries. I got so busy answering questions, I found it challenging to return to my other work. My number of speaking engagements about Bj 581 soared into the stratosphere. Soon Neil Price and I were lecturing about the "female Viking warrior" all over the world. It didn't seem real.

The paper received a lot of high fives, but it also got its share of smackdowns. In fact, some critics were fierce and unsparing. The media outlets spanned from international news formats like CNN, the *New York Times*, the *Washington Post*, and *Newsweek*, to business publications like *Forbes*, to scientific periodicals like *Science* magazine and *National Geographic*. Each article bore a headline that attracted the attention of even non–Viking lovers.

- **FIRST FEMALE VIKING WARRIOR PROVED THROUGH DNA:**
  "This finding should make all archaeologists question previous

identifications of the sex of Viking warriors." —Kristina Killgrove, *Forbes*, September 8, 2017

- VIKING WARRIOR DISCOVERED IN SWEDEN WAS A WOMAN, RESEARCHERS CONFIRM: "These latest findings, the researchers write, 'prove a new understanding of the Viking society, the social constructions and also norms in the Viking Age.'" —Emily Shugerman, *INKL*, September 8, 2017

- THIS VIKING DNA DISCOVERY IS OUR BEST EVIDENCE TO DATE OF FEMALE VIKING WARRIORS: "Still, while one discovery can't tell us how common female combatants are, having DNA evidence confirming at least one instance of a prominent warrior-class woman is a sign that the stories weren't all fantasy." —Mike McRae, *Just Good News*, September 9, 2017

- FAMOUS VIKING WARRIOR WAS A WOMAN, DNA REVEALS: "'It was held up before as a kind of "ideal" male warrior grave,' says Baylor University archaeologist Davide Zori, who wasn't involved with the research. 'It's possible, albeit unlikely, that the woman's relatives buried her with a warrior's equipment without that having been her role in life.' Given available evidence, though, Zori says he's fairly confident in the study's results." —Michael Greshko, *National Geographic*, September 12, 2017

- DOES NEW DNA EVIDENCE PROVE THAT THERE WERE FEMALE VIKING WARLORDS? "'It is exciting because the traditional images of Vikings are masculine and war hungry—with the women at home baking or looking after the kids,' says Becky Gowland, a lecturer in archaeology at Durham University in Durham, England. 'This burial is clearly of a high-status woman. It doesn't indicate that she's a warrior, but if we interpret [male graves] in that way, why not women as well?' So how many more warrior bones have been presumed male that might be female? In Poland, 'archaeology is really getting to grips with a number

of anomalous graves,' according to Carolyne Larrington, professor of medieval European literature at Oxford University."
—Paula Cocozza, *The Guardian*, September 12, 2017

- **SKELETON IGNITES VIKING WARRIOR DEBATE:** "'Have
we found the Mulan of Sweden, or a woman buried with the
rank symbols of a husband who died abroad?' asks archaeologist Søren Sindbæk of Aarhus University, Denmark."
—Bruce Bower, *Science News Digital*, October 14, 2017

ARCHAEOLOGICAL REACTIONS

In addition to the press coverage, there was broad academic comment. In the time before the Internet, other academics would
likely have written articles in response and put them through the
peer-review process. But in this instant, online world, most of the
reactions came in tweets and blogs.

Some of the supporting comments included:

- **Marianne Moen, archaeologist, University of Oslo and Museum
of Cultural History:** "When you find a woman [buried with]
weapons, you have to think about what this means for this particular person, for society at large and for men, if women could have
these roles as well. We need to start thinking about [gender roles]
as a bit more fluid and less strict and stop talking about men and
women in different ways when they are buried in the same way."

- **Carolyne Larrington, professor of Medieval European literature at the University of Oxford:** "We are getting quite a lot
of evidence that the gender roles may have been more fluid in
the Viking period than we thought, and that it's quite possible
women may have been regarded as socially male even though
biologically they weren't—and might have been able to assume
positions of military leadership. We don't tend to imagine
women sitting on the longships, but they must have been there."

Others raised questions that the team anticipated. In fact, the team foresaw most of the issues and included their views on them in the paper.

> Do weapons necessarily determine a warrior? The interpretation of grave goods is not straight forward, but it must be stressed that the interpretation should be made in a similar manner regardless of the biological sex of the interred individual.
>
> Similar associations of women buried with weapons have been dismissed, arguing that the armaments could have been heirlooms, carriers of symbolic meaning or grave goods reflecting the status and role of the family rather than the individual ([Leszek] Gardeła, 2013). Male individuals in burials with a similar material record are not questioned in the same way. Furthermore, an argument can be put forward that the grave originally may have held a second, now missing, individual. In which case, the weaponry could have been a part of that individual's grave furnishings, while the remaining female was buried without any objects.

However, this did not stop some literary, historical, anthropological, and archaeological critics from claiming some harsh and surprising things. Some were interviewed by the international press, some blogged, some tweeted, and a few submitted articles for peer review.

- **Judith Jesch, runologist, Old Icelandic literature expert, and professor at the University of Nottingham:** Jesch specializes in Old Norse language, literature, and runology and is the author of at least two books and several articles that address Viking women and female warriors. On her blog, *Norse and Viking Ramblings*, she appeared rankled from the start that she was cited by the team as "generally dismissing women warriors as mythological phenomena." While it may be true that her earlier book suggests women warriors were "generally mythological phenomenon" (and she stands by that), in her newer book, from 2015, *The Viking Diaspora*, she expressly observes what humans are capable of:

> What these examples [from Viking literature] show is that people in the Viking Age and its aftermath were perfectly capable of imaging women as warriors, or at least as imagining them as carrying and using weapons, whether this occurred in real life or not. Doubtless it did occur in real life, since human beings are capable of most things, whether or not it is considered "normal" for them to do so, but the strong emphasis on gender distinctions in Viking Age society . . . suggests that it did not happen very often.

In her blog post, she recited a long list of criticisms of the article, including that the team failed to "confirm" they had found a female Viking warrior as the title suggested, used an Icelandic poem without consideration of its deeper literary context, had no support for saying the person in the grave was a "high-ranking officer," failed to properly address the absence of traumatic injury on the bones or the disarray of the Birka collection, and couldn't show the bones tested actually belonged to the grave. Additionally, she asserted that the team was at fault for not raising hypothetical scenarios for alternate consideration, such as, *the weapons in the grave may have belonged to the female's husband* [emphasis added].

- **Fedir Androshchuk, archaeologist:** Androshchuk wrote a peer-reviewed article in response. In his paper, "Female Viking Revisited," published in *Viking and Medieval Scandinavia* in 2018, he points out what he believes were flaws in the authors' archaeological method. These include: not fully acknowledging the disturbed state of the Birka graves; Stolpe's nonprofessionals (farmers) doing some of the excavation, note-taking, and draw-ings; differences between the original sketch and later interpretive sketches of the grave; the absence of Stolpe from the site for some periods and his reliance on the notes and reports of his men; the potential effect of stone removal on the underlying grave con-tents; and the team's lack of full exploration of the osteological reports. He believed Berit Vilkans's records showed the presence of a second body, and Kjellström's article memorialized the jum-bled state of the boxes. He then recited facts of other graves in other locations with similar physical contents and qualities that he strongly believed contained both a man and a woman.

To sum up, Androshchuk wrote, "I completely concur with the general view and presumption concerning the passive role of women during the Viking Age should be reconsidered." How-ever, he added that grave Bj 581 should not have been chosen for DNA testing. He concluded that the geneticists effectively didn't know what they were testing, and it cannot be said that the bones, even if from the Bj 581 and even if a female, do not prove that the person was the sole body in the grave. *There had to have been a male body in the grave at some point, buried perhaps at a later time* [emphasis added].

- **Martin Rundkvist, archaeologist:** Rundkvist weighed in on his blog *Aardvarchaeology* saying, "Your skeleton can't tell us anything about your gender, and your grave goods can't tell us anything about your osteo-sex [*sex as determined your by bones*] . . . [but] mismatches between osteo-sex and artifact gender are extremely rare. . . . But now we have one. . . . The plan of the grave shows which bones were well preserved. This should be enough to counter the charge that maybe the skeleton currently labelled Bj 581 is not in fact the one found in this weapon grave. This the authors should have written a few sentences about. I take their silence to mean that having already published her arguments about this elsewhere, Kjellström considers the issue uncontroversial. . . . We still can't rule out the early removal of an articulated male body. But such an argument ex silentio would demand that we place similar female bodies in all other weapon graves as well. We can't just create the bodies we want in order for the material to look neat."

In an interview with *Science* magazine, Hedenstierna-Jonson replied to many of the comments about grave interpretation, "Well, that's the key question: How do we interpret a grave? That's something we always face in archaeology. What does a grave represent? Asking whether the person buried ever fought in battle is a relevant question, but this has been known as a warrior grave since the 1880s and nobody has questioned it before. Nobody has made that comment before they knew the bones were from a woman. The archaeology has not changed. The only thing that has changed is our knowledge that it's a woman and not a man."

To all the criticism, the team repeated again and again that their interpretation was based on the DNA test of the same person uncovered by Stolpe. In other words, nothing had changed from the long-held view that the person in grave Bj 581 was a high-ranking Viking warrior, except that they used contemporary methods to more accurately identify the sex.

They pointed to the science of the DNA testing and the fact that ancient Scandinavian skeletal remains are tested in special labs with chemical, biological, physical, and geological analytical methods applicable to the individual preservation.

From the team's perspective, the dialogue should have been moving on to a multidisciplinary discussion of how the DNA results provide a new window into Viking society and long-held beliefs about females, rather than more generalizations and inventions of facts that did not exist. In their view, the DNA results called for more than a social media blizzard of feelings and impressions mixed with some facts randomly cited here and there.

They wholly supported a detailed discussion of the research in the context of the full range of Viking Age research: science, literature, and history.

8

WARRIORS, WEAPONS, AND WOMEN

ALMOST ALL SCHOLARS AGREE that Old Norse literature *and* archaeology (among other areas of study) are needed to fully grasp the roles of Viking women and their relationship to weapons and warfare. And it is not possible to understand one without studying the other.

OLD NORSE LITERATURE

The Vikings had numerous tales and poems of kings, battles, fierce women, families, slaves, dragons, and other creatures. These stories are often described collectively as "Old Norse literature" or "texts." They are filled with action and colorful detail, but it has to be remembered that they weren't written down during Viking times. Except for short runic inscriptions, the only Scandinavian texts that exist today come from the Middle Ages and later—two centuries and more *after* the Viking Age.

As entertaining and valuable as they are, they cannot be considered the truth of what actually occurred. Still, archaeologists refer to them when they are interpreting artifacts and context, just as historians point to archaeological finds that match up with events in the works.

Why would they do this? It's a delicate business, connecting the artifact and fictional worlds of the Vikings. The full range of material includes runic inscriptions, skaldic poetry, poems with mythological or heroic themes, a fascinating handbook known as the *Prose Edda* that refers to poetry and mythology, an anthology of old poetry known as the *Poetic Edda*, the many genres of the Icelandic sagas, Latin sources such as the *Gesta Danorum*, laws, and more.

They sometimes mention recognizable places. They sometimes tell of items and events that match up to artifacts. But most of all, the characters have the kind of passion, devotion, fervor, and rage that we associate with living, breathing humans.

Runic inscriptions, which were created during the Viking Age, are one of the few written sources that were inscribed by the Vikings themselves. They were made using an alphabet where the characters look like branches and twigs. They appear on stones, wood, jewelry, weapons, and other items.

There are over 6,700 runic inscriptions from Scandinavia and its colonies (Britain, Greenland, etc.). There are two runic alphabets and several different forms of runes, including a more formal version called *long-branch runes* and a more casual version called *short-twig runes*. They require particular skill to interpret. Runic inscriptions on stone are often more about the people making the memorial than the ones they are remembering.

Skaldic poetry or **skaldic verse** was created and passed down orally during the Viking Age, but for the most part it was not written down until the thirteenth century by Icelanders. The skald poet stood before the chieftain and the public and recited the poem in lyric metaphors with complicated meter and metaphorical nouns and phrases called *kennings*. Despite this gap in recording it, most skaldic poetry experts believe that the verse has survived essentially intact since the Viking Age. This is so because the poems use a verse form that lends itself to memorization.

The ***Poetic Edda*** is a term scholars use for a collection of poetry that actually comes from several different manuscripts. It's a body of heroic and mythological verse that incorporates comedy, tragedy, satire, and high drama. Themes in the *Poetic Edda* have inspired famous artists including Richard Wagner, C. S. Lewis, and J. R. R. Tolkien. The bulk of the poems are found in a volume from the 1270s and known as the *Codex Regius*. In addition to the poems in the *Codex Regius*, there are other poems that are considered part of the Eddic tradition because they tackle similar subjects in a similar way.

The **Prose Edda**, written by Snorri Sturluson in the thirteenth century, includes snippets of some of the same poems as are found in the *Poetic Edda*. The broad content of Snorri's *Prose Edda* is to discuss the art of poetry in a technical way and often refers to the myths and heroic legends of the Scandinavians as suitable subject matter. Because of the time that he wrote it, it pays some respect to Christianity. Christianity entered the Viking realm during the last half of the Viking Age and was well established in Snorri's time.

Snorri Sturluson, as imagined by Norwegian painter, professor, writer, and journalist *Christian Krohg,* in 1899. *Wikimedia Commons*

The **Icelandic sagas**, of which there are dozens, are a collection of tales about the Vikings, sometimes incorporating skaldic verse, that date back seven hundred years or more. No one knows how true these stories are since they were passed down through spoken word and were not written down until approximately three hundred years after the events supposedly took place. Some of the stories were even invented in the medieval period.

VIKING WARRIORS

Warriors have a looming presence in Viking literature. One thing that we know is that warfare was part of everyday life for Viking Age people. It affected everyone. Even people who did not actively participate in conflict had some part in the activity of warring.

Conflict erupted in varied forms. Wars to defend families were common. Disputes within communities and kingdoms raged, and there was warring and raiding that they inflicted on non-Viking people. There were those who fought on the ground in hand-to-hand combat, those who rode horseback and wielded weapons from that higher vantage point, those who supported the warriors on their ships and in their camps, those who made the weapons and the clothing, those who built the longships and made the sails, those who instigated the conflicts, those who strategized the movements, those who acted as pagan and magical consultants to decision makers, and so much more.

Young children probably watched in awe as the embattled, scarred, but proud warriors arrived home from a campaign over land or sea, hauling their prizes and touting their wealth and success. Some youngsters must have looked forward to the day they too could have their own horse or go on a longship to raid and trade. They may have looked forward to it because it was a natural path to wealth, even though being a warrior was not for the squeamish. They may also have noticed a change to the personalities of some of the warriors who returned traumatized by what they had seen and done.

Runic Inscriptions Tell of Battles

Runic inscriptions were etched on stones and are typically a formula: X raises this stone for Y (his/her father/mother, son/daughter, leader/king). On a warrior's stone, the inscription includes information about the warrior's battles and military adventures. The inscriptions also tell something about social roles of warriors and the "warrior ideal." They mention rank and status and tell of the "war band," which the warrior had signed up to defend. War bands could be family related, commercial and trading related, kingdom related, or any other group position where a warrior cast his allegiance and was compensated.

The common runic phrase used for bravery and group loyalty (as translated by the Victorians) is that "the warrior fled not." Modern translations are less poetic: *He didn't run away*, or *He fought while he could hold weapons*, or *He kept on killing as long as he could hold weapons.*

Not all runic inscriptions are fancy and praising. Some are casual. A mid-twentieth century discovery at Bergen and Trondheim, Norway, recovered hundreds of medieval, water-preserved wooden slips inscribed with runes with a variety of mundane purposes: merchants' tallies, shopping lists, name tags of ownership ("Sigmund owns this sack"), and scrawls ("Things are bad with me, partner. I did not get the beer or the fish. . . ."), among other things.

Skaldic Poetry Also Praises Warriors

The skaldic praise poem *Haraldskvæði* contains the earliest Norse literary reference to some of the most violent warriors—the berserkers. Composed by Þórbjörn Hornklofi, the poem describes the Battle of Hafrsfjörðr in 872 CE:

> They [Harald's ships] were loaded with farmer-chiefs and broad shields, with Vestland spear and Frankish sword: *berserkir* screamed, the battle was on, *ulfheðnar* howled and shook their spears.
>
> Of the berserkr-fury I would ask, about the drinkers of the corpse-sea [blood]: what are they like, these men who go happy into battle?
>
> *Ulfheðnar* they are called, who bear bloody shields in the slaughter; they redden spears when they join the fighting: there they are arranged for their task; there I know that the honorable prince places his trust only in brave men, who hack at shields.

Skaldic verse expert Judith Jesch explains in her article "Constructing the Warrior Ideal in the Late Viking Age" how children were prepared for the profession of warrior. It wasn't lessons so much as impressions that were made to young minds. Verses praise warriors for feeding the beasts of battle, the carrion eaters: the raven, the eagle, and the wolf. In the literal sense, this is the same as not fleeing since staying to fight leaves corpses on the field, and these attract the carrion eaters.

Berserk

The current day word *berserk*, defined as "being out of control with anger, frenzied, or excited" derives from the Norse word *berserkr*. "When they lost the game, she went berserk, throwing things around the room."

When there are references in the poems to those who flee, it is always the enemies who are the cowards. In the official praise poetry of the chieftain, the warriors who belong to the war band would never flee, so the victor is praised for making his opponent flee. The *not fleeing* theme is also used as a heroic description of the loser who stays on the field and dies.

Most experts consider this all to be an ideal since there must have been tactical military retreats. Its purpose must have been to indoctrinate young warriors to overcome their instinct to save themselves by running away in fear and/or their innate resistance to killing other human beings.

A battlefield would have been a fearful and unpleasant place, filled with dead bodies, blood, guts, gore, carrion eaters, and the threat of one's own death. The bravery and courage associated with feeding the beasts of battle is one of compensation and reward. This is also reflected in Eddic poetry and the sagas.

Eddic Poetry Tells of a Battle from the Warrior's Perspective
Egill Skallagrimsson (tenth century)
[#2] *The poet remembers battles in Sweden*

> I went with bloody sword
> (wound-grouse following me)
> and a resounding spear
> to a hard viking attack.

We had a raging fight,
fire raced over houses;
I made bloody bodies
Fall within city walls.

Wound-grouse = raven

Sagas Were Filled with Warriors' Escapades

The sagas are filled with epic stories of fighting for revenge, land, fame, love, wealth—fighting for your own team and fighting as a mercenary.

Once committed to a chieftain, prince, or king, a warrior became part of that person's retinue and was regarded as part of the household. They swore oaths of allegiance, and most leaders preferred to sign them up when they were young. In the *Saga of Olav Haraldsson*, the king receives the following advice from his counsel:

> We have a big enough army, but the people assembled here are great men and chiefs. Young men are not worse in warfare; they want to win wealth and status. Also, when chieftains go into battle it is their custom to have many men going in front as a shield for themselves, but it is often the case that people who have little money fight better than those who have grown up in wealth.

In addition to the vigor of youth, the sagas also speak of the extreme violence of the berserkers. The social and psychological behavior of this type of fighter is described by Snorri Sturluson in *Ynglingasaga*:

> Óðinn could bring it about that in battle his opponents were struck with blindness or deafness or panic, and their weapons would cut no better than sticks, while his men went without mail and were as wild as dogs or wolves, biting their shields, being as strong as bears or

bulls. They killed the people, but neither fire nor iron took effect on them. That is called berserk fury.

ARCHAEOLOGY AND WARRIORS

In archaeology, there are similar "weapon dancer" images of men who were either naked or clad in wolf pelts and wildly wielding swords and spears. They also appear in metalwork, textiles, and runestones. Some of the images depict them with masks of dogs or bulls. According to Roderick Dale, "the term berserksgangr (generally translated as 'going berserk') literally describes a way of moving, 'berserk-walking,' and not a fighting rage at all—something that might fit well with the strangely formal postures of the 'weapon dancers' and the pelt-wearing warriors on the metalwork."

Neil Price describes the *literary* berserkers as "stock villains—useful antagonists for the heroes to kill—although in the kings' sagas they are sometimes present as regular parts of the royal retinue, a sort of Viking special forces."

In the time before the Viking Age, Scandinavian people had contact with northern Europe through trade and piracy but on a smaller scale. No one knows exactly what kicked off the brutal raids that marked the start of the Viking Age. Some scholars say that only a small proportion of the population were warriors. Others disagree. Almost all researchers concur that the raids were motivated by a desire to gain wealth and status.

Why the extreme brutality? Some say that Viking warriors' reputation for brutality has been exaggerated. Not that they weren't brutal—they have a few recorded methods of killing people that are stomach turning. But they were no more brutal than their Christian contemporaries. Brutality can be described in more than one way. It can be physical action on a raid, and it can be the extensive trading in humans as slaves, a brutality that is not exaggerated.

In her book, *The Viking Age: A Time of Many Faces,* Caroline Ahlström Arcini, who has extensively examined Viking skeletons, writes:

The Viking Age is known for being a violent period. The osteological results show surprisingly few traces of violence, whether healed or not. Was the strategy that they used when raiding to attack people who were unprepared and therefore unarmed? Or is the reason that the Vikings were on the warpath more in the early Viking Age, when people in Scandinavia mostly cremated their dead, with the result that we cannot identify traces of healed injuries? Is there anything to indicate slaves were treated badly, that they have more healed fractures than other people? The great problem here is the difficulty of identifying individuals who belonged to the group of slaves. . . . There is nothing to suggest that the frequency of fractures or weapon related violence was greater than in, say, the Middle Ages; if anything, it was lower.

THE *LIÐ*

The literature describes Viking warrior groups that acted as "bands of brothers." These groups were formed of professional warriors from all across Scandinavia who swore allegiance to one person, who in turn promised to feed, clothe, and arm them. The word for the group was *lið*. It could have as few as two ships full of warriors or as many as two hundred. They were not necessarily friends or neighbors, but their efforts demanded high levels of cooperation and coordination. Some were considered generals or commanders who, when they went to the field, participated directly in battle.

Sometimes they did not return home. They died in battle, became settlers, or switched sides and became mercenary fighters against other Vikings. But it was one way to gain portable wealth, afford to marry, and perhaps own land. Men with few marriage prospects at home might take women captive as wives by force while they were on raids.

An Example of a *Lið*

Around the year 750 CE, a band of Viking warriors from Sweden dragged two longships onto an island off the coast of Estonia in what is now the village of Salme. They had just retrenched after a bloody raid. One of the ships carried the corpses of forty of their Viking peers, including their king. They all bore stabbing, slicing, and hacking wounds. The survivors attempted to reassemble the body parts into the larger ship, cover them with their weapons and shields, and build a makeshift burial mound.

In 2008, workers laying electrical cable discovered the ship, and archaeologists now know a great deal more about these Viking warriors. Before this find, archaeologists believed that a ship would have a few high-status warriors, each with a collection of weapons, and the rest would be farmers armed with axes and perhaps swords. But all the warriors on these ships appeared to be well equipped and of higher status.

VIKING WEAPONS AND GRAVES

Archaeologists have found many intact graves from the Viking Age that contain weapons. Weapons are also referred to extensively in Viking literature.

Runic Inscriptions About and on the Weapons Themselves

Runic inscriptions mention weapons and their complex association with people. Inscriptions were also carved on the weapons themselves. Pattern forging, inscriptions, and cryptic symbols such as omegas, circles, and crosses on sword blades were certainly seen as quality marks but can also be interpreted as bestowing spiritual properties on the weapon.

Skaldic Poetry and Weapons

In skaldic poetry, there are 350 different ways to say *weapon*. The most widespread form of poetic description is the kenning. A kenning is a metaphorical compound word or phrase that replaces a single noun. For example, rather than saying "blood," one might say "battle sweat."

Descriptions and names of famous swords, spears, axes, and other weapons were kennings. There are over 3,500 kennings for describing weapons and how they inflicted pain or represented power in Old Norse literature. Sometimes they are not so short. A verse by Þórðr Særeksson (Sjáreksson), from his poem "Þórálfs drápa Skólmssonar," uses this kenning: "the slinger of the fire of the storm of the troll-woman of the shielding moon of the horse of boathouses."

Sagas and Weapons

The sagas wouldn't be the sagas without weapons. While the main action in sagas is battle, it isn't all slash, hack, burn, and berserkers. As much as the men and women who carried them, swords had personalities and were revered for their accomplishments. They even acquired names. In Egil's saga, Egil Skalla-Grímsson had Dragvandil, a blade that was reputed to be so long it dragged on the ground. Other named blades in the sagas and poems include: Legbiter; Stream of Anguish; Wrath; Hrunting the dragon-killer; Skofnung, the sword that bound the souls of twelve berserkers; and Tyrfing, the sword forged by dwarves with a blade that shone like flames.

Archaeology and Weapons

Kim Hjardar and Vegard Vike explain that the design and elegance of a weapon, particularly a sword, enhanced the owner's prestige and helped build political relationships. "The ideal weapon almost came to life when it was taken up for battle, like a snake ready to strike or a carnivore who has scented blood."

In *Children of Ash and Elm*, Neil Price busts the myth that Vikings are only about slashing and hacking. "The effective use of Viking weaponry relied very much on more than brute force, the opposite of the crude barbarian cliché still propagated so widely." Each weapon required different skills, and men would train from a young age, learning the qualities of each. "To use them in combination was a kind of lethal dance, a choreographed interplay of movement, balance, dexterity, and strength—all while wielding deadly tools to cut or pierce."

- **Axes** were the most common and basic tool and usually the first weapon a Viking acquired. Many found in Viking burials are coarse and heavy and more like working tools than weapons. However, for warriors they were not household axes but rather longer-handled and heavier-headed, with more vicious cutting edges. They were used both while on foot and while on horseback. In the same way that swords acquired names, so did axes. Ax names were in the feminine form and refer to aggression and rage. Ax names such as "aggressive old hag troll," "outlawed old hag troll," and "shield seeker and shield wrecker" are found in the sagas and skaldic poetry.

Copper alloy figurine showing a rider and a standing figure. Images of this kind have been conventionally interpreted as representations of Valkyries.
Courtesy of Leszek Gardeła

- **Spears** were of different lengths with spearheads of varying widths. The heads were riveted to the shaft. Some were elaborately decorated. They could be used in close combat, from a distance on foot, or from horseback. "The slimmest lances had lean, pointed profiles and ash shafts of up to two metres [6.6

feet], suited for a clean cast or mounted charge. The heavier varieties had thicker heads and wider blades, sufficient to cause deep, broad, penetrating wounds."

- **Swords** were the ultimate signs of warrior prestige, and they were also the most expensive to acquire. According to Price, "Swords were slashing weapons, designed to cut rather than stab. . . . Most sword hilts ended in a heavy pommel, the best of them made to exactly counterbalance the weight of the blade." They were considered an object of beauty, and they are described in poetry as having snakes writhing in the iron. Decorations, including images and runes, were carved on the hilt and its parts: the guard, the pommel, and the grip.

- **Scabbards**, the sheaths that covered the swords, were made of wood panels lined with greased wool and were sometimes covered in leather or metal. A metal chape protected the pointed end. The scabbard was either suspended horizontally from a belt or worn on a cross-body strap. The scabbard could be decorated, with the most intricate decorations reserved for the highest-status warriors.

Boat Burials

The Viking Salme boat burials were unusual in that archaeologists found more swords than warriors. Experts offer a variety of possible explanations: the additional swords could have been burial gifts, stand-ins for warriors whose bodies were not retrievable, or part of individuals' personal stashes—all the weapons they owned in life following them into death.

- **Battle knives** or **fighting knives** were single-edged blade knives that made a short, stabbing blow. They could be used to cut throats and rip chests. Experts believe them to be a backup weapon. They sometimes had elaborate scabbards worn at the waist so they could be drawn with a cross-body motion. They hung from a harness or were worn on the back.

- **Bows and arrows** were part of the full set of weapons. Made of a straight piece of ash that is bent and strung, bows could be used standing or while on a horse. The arrowheads varied. Some tips were broad and blunted to cause serious wounds to unprotected flesh, and others were sharp and pointed so they could get into chain mail.

- **Shields** had a core material of wood and were generally covered in leather and centered with a raised iron boss decoration on the outside and a handle on the inside. Sometimes shields bore designs for individuals, sometimes they had a group designation, and other times they were of a plain color. Warriors overlapped their shields to form a wall or carried them on the side of a horse to protect the horse's flank.

- **Armor** consisted of quilted jackets, padded leather, or chain mail made of thousands of interlocking rings. Chain mail could be short and vestlike or long to the ankle. In the Baltic area, there is evidence of armor made of rectangular plates of iron.

- **Helmets** are presumed to have been worn by most warriors, but only one complete example has ever been found. It surfaced at Gjermundbu in Norway. It's an iron skullcap with a nose protector and eye guard. Chain mail most likely covered the rest of the face and neck. Images of similar helmets have been seen carved into stones and three-dimensional sculptures. None of the helmets had horns.

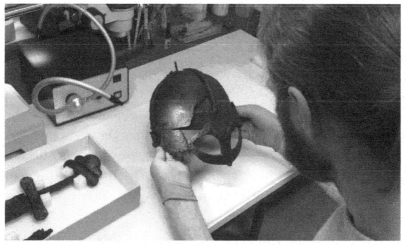

Conservation work being done on the only Viking helmet so far ever recovered. In 2018 Vegard Vike tweeted: "Today I started conservation work on the Gjermundbu helmet—sometimes referred to as the only #Viking Helmet. The process will entail disassembly, micro-sandblasting, detailed photos of all parts, X-ray, 3D-scan and a new mounting."
Courtesy of Jessica Leigh McGraw

- **Personal knives** were available to almost everyone but were not considered weapons. In battle they would have been used as a last resort. Knives were occasionally given to a slave who was being freed as an expression of a new life. A slave, however, could only own a small personal knife intended for tasks.

Interpreting Weapons in Graves

A large part of interpreting the life of an excavated person is evaluating their grave goods. Weapons are evaluated by their kind (sword, spear, ax, shield, bow, arrowheads, etc.), their number, their placement in the grave, and by comparison to other graves with weapons. Additionally, archaeologists consider whether the weapons actually belonged to the person or persons in the grave and for what purpose they were used.

The full consideration includes any battle wear on the weapons, where the weapons might have originated, if they were acquired during extensive travel, whether they might have been gifts, and so on.

Since Stolpe's time, archaeologists have changed their opinions about weapons in graves. They no longer automatically assume weapons mean a male grave; neither do they automatically conclude weapons mean a warrior grave. Some experts also believe that to label a grave with weapons as a "warrior grave" is to jump to the conclusion that the person inside was personally engaged in the occupation of warring.

This is not to say that the person was *not* a warrior. However, analysis has reached a finer level of detail. As a result, the terminology that Stolpe used, "warrior grave," would not automatically be applied to a grave excavated today that has a one or more weapons. Archaeologists might not even consider sex at first but might begin by assigning the term "weapon grave," until the significance of the weapons can be determined.

It is possible in some circumstances to determine the wear and tear on the weapons beyond corrosion caused by excavation. Any dents or jagged edges (and sometimes blood) found can assist in interpreting their actual use in combat. Modern technologies such as neutron scanning are applied when budgets allow. But many experts agree that wear and tear on weapons is not a sole criteria for interpreting a grave as that of a warrior.

At some point, however, the type and number of weapons in a grave will lend themselves to an interpretation that the person in the grave really was a warrior.

WOMEN AND WEAPONS AND GRAVES

Stolpe and other early archaeologists did not have the benefit of osteological testing. They tended to assume sex on the basis of what they found in the graves. The outcome, in turn, depended on what they themselves associated with those objects.

In societies where women were generally confined to household roles, domestic goods and jewelry in a grave meant the person was female. Similarly, where warring was associated with men, weapons in a grave meant "male." This, of course, presented a problem when cooking utensils and jewelry showed up in what they would ordinarily classify as a male grave.

Archaeologists recognize this dilemma. However, experts today tend to agree that the core conclusion—weapon graves are male—is probably correct for a large part of the Viking population. Still, since the 1980s, archaeology and Norse literature studies have increasingly widened their view of women in Viking society. Women are viewed as more than keepers of the home fires, and using weapons in a fighting environment is not ruled out for them.

A literary history of weapon-wielding and warring women exists. Some of it is helpful to uncovering the facts; some of it not. Contemporary culture has unfortunately exploded the ideas and images of fighting Viking women beyond their literary and actual realities. It is hard to set aside many of the comic book, cartoon, movie, TV, and advertising conceptualizations of Valkyries and shield-maidens, but it's important to do so in order to place them in their proper perspective relative to real Viking women who may have taken up arms.

Valkyries

The word *valkyria* in old Norse means "chooser of the slain." The legends tell of women who were servants of the god Odin, the highest god, who were sent into battles to select warriors who would be taken to *Valhöll*, a sort of Viking afterlife. The chosen would be served mead and live to fight alongside the gods in the final cosmic war *Ragnarök*. The Valkyries rode on flying horses from the skies onto battlefields where they made their choices, bestowing the honor of victory or agony of defeat on individual warriors.

Valkyries in Sagas and Poetry

An anonymous poem that is quoted in Njál's saga, the *Darraðarljóð*, "The Song of the Spears" is a gruesome twelve-stanza story about supernatural women who are described in an introduction as Valkyries. The poem tells of the 1014 Battle of Clontarf between the Irish King Brian Boru and his warriors on one side, and the Scandinavian Vikings of Ireland and the Western Isles of Orkney and Mann on the other. In the poem, the Valkyries are engaged in two activities simultaneously: weaving a weft of war, or a fabric made of men's intestines, and describing (even directing) the battle. They use sharp weapons and weight the fabric with skulls, causing the combatants' blood to flow onto the battlefield. The idea of the poem is that the Valkyries weave the performance of war.

Valkyries named Hild, Hjorthrimul, Sanngrid, and Svipul, among others, weave the war. An excerpt from the blood-drenched verse tells it all:

> The warp is woven
> with warriors' guts,
> and heavily weighted
> with the heads of men.
> Spears serve as heddle rods,
> spattered with blood;
> Iron-bound is the shed rod,
> and arrows are the pin beaters;
> we will beat with swords
> our battle web.

Most scholars agree that as the handmaidens of Odin, Valkyries were not mere visitors to the battlefield or choosers but were metaphors for war.

Jóhanna Katrín Friðriksdóttir, author of *Valkyrie: The Women of the Viking World*, agrees. "In a figurative sense, valkyries could even be understood as having their roots here, being the personification of the spears and arrows that 'choose' the slain."

The translation of their names reveals their chilling purpose: Göndul, the "War-Fetter"; Hlökk, the "Chain," "Mist," or "Cloud"; Hjalmthrimul, "Helmet-Clatter"; Hjörthrimul, "Sword-Noise";

Hjlód, "Howling"; Randgnithr, "Shield-Scraper"; Skalmjöld, "Sword-Time"; Sváva, "Killer"; and Tanngnithr, "Teeth-Grinder." Their sisters' names include Battle-Weaver, Shaker, Disorder, Scent-of-Battle, Victory-Froth, Vibration, Unstable, Treader, Swan-White, Shield-Destroyer, Helper, Armour, Devastate, and Silence.

Given their literary, metaphorical existence and their supernatural powers, Valkyries are not a particularly persuasive source of evidence that there were honest-to-goodness human female Viking warriors. They were created to inspire the *feel* of battle. The Victorians further imagined them with horned helmets, and current framers have morphed them into hypersexualized pop culture characters to populate video games and movies. With each commercial incarnation they become less and less Viking-like—and certainly less human.

Shield-Maidens

Shield-maidens are very different from Valkyries, even though the terms are often used interchangeably. They materialize most often as real women who don't merely carry shields and swords; they fight in battles alongside men. There are not a large number of them, but they are there.

- **Shield-maidens and the *Saga of Hervor and Heidrek*:** Two famous shield-maidens of the same name appear in the legendary *Saga of Hervor and Heidrek* from the thirteenth and fourteenth centuries. The saga tells of the Tyrfing, a cursed sword that must draw blood before it can be sheathed again.

    Hervor the elder (the grandmother), when she is young, is angered by being called the daughter of a pig herder and is inspired to go on a Viking expedition. She doesn't want anything to do with sewing and other "girl" tasks and instead learns archery, swordsmanship, and horse riding. She dresses like a man and, using the name Hjörvard, she fights, kills, and pillages with the men using the name Hjörvard. Later in life, she grows tired of the fighting life and abandons it. She picks

Hervor the second
dying in battle.
Peter Nicolai Arbor,
Wikimedia Commons

up an embroidery project, marries, has children, and leads a
more typical female domestic life. She has two sons and eventually a granddaughter, also named Hervor, who becomes the
commander of a Gothic fort and inherits her father's sword
and status. She falls in battle against the Huns. Hervor the second (granddaughter) lived her life fully in the role of a warrior, while Hervor the first changed from a warrior to a more
domestic female.

- **Shield-maiden Lathgertha:** One of the most notable
  shield-maidens is Lathgertha. She appears in the *Gesta Dano-*
  rum, a twelfth-century work by Danish historian Saxo Grammaticus. When the Swedish King Frey invades Norway and
  imprisons many of the women of the Norwegian king's family,
  Lathgertha and the other women dress like men and fight alongside Ragnar Lodbrok, who is leading the male forces defending
  Norway. She has the courage of a man and a determination to
  fight bravely on the front lines. Lathgertha marries Ragnar, is
  divorced by him, and remarries another king, whom she slays
  in a quarrel. She apparently preferred to rule alone rather than
  share the throne.

  Lathgertha is not believed to have been a real historical
  person. The first nine volumes of the history, where Lathgertha
  is mentioned, are considered to be fictional tales of mythical

Lathgertha imagined in a 1913 lithograph.
Morris Meredith Williams, Wikimedia Commons

Norse figures. In Volume VII Saxo Grammaticus reveals the expected role of women of his time by describing proper Viking women juxtaposed against this rough warring lifestyle.

> There were once women in Denmark who dressed themselves to look like men and spent almost every

minute cultivating soldiers' skills; they did not want to allow the sinews of their valour to lose tautness and be infected by self-indulgence. Loathing a dainty style of living, they would harden body and mind with endurance and toil, rejecting all the fickle pliancy of girls and compelling their womanish natures to act with a virile ruthlessness. They courted military expertise so earnestly that anyone would have guessed they had unsexed themselves. Those especially who had forceful personalities or were tall and elegant tended to embark on this way of life. As if they were forgetful of their true selves they put toughness before allure, aimed at conflicts instead of kisses, tasted blood, not lips, sought the clash of arms rather than the arms of embrace, fitted to weapons hands which should have been weaving, desired not the couch but the kills, and those they could have appeased with looks they attacked with lances.

In 2012, the character Lagertha (based on Lathgertha) burst onto the contemporary cultural scene with no superpowers but with impressive warrior qualities. The History Channel series *Vikings*, created and written by Michael Hirst, was inspired by the *Saga of Ragnar Lodbrok*, and Hirst has commented that he made a purposeful choice to amplify the shield-maiden characters in his series.

Origin of the Word Shield-Maiden

Old Norse literature expert Judith Jesch conducted what she described as a "verbal archaeology" of the term *shield-maiden*. Her article "Women, War and Words: A Verbal Archaeology of

Shield-Maidens," analyzes the vocabulary used in both history and literature to represent women acting in the traditionally male role of warrior and traces the term to its possible origins.

She focuses on the Old Norse term *skjaldmær*, which translates as *shield-maiden*, and the use of this word as opposed to all the other terms that have been, or are being, used: *female Viking, female Viking warrior, warrior woman, Amazon, armed female, Valkyrie*, and equivalents in other languages. And she explores whether the textual term, in fact, can lead to real shield-maidens.

Ultimately, she finds the word *skjaldmær* has no origin of its own in the Norse context but is an Old Norse coinage (or invention) based on the classical idea of the fearsome fighting women called *Amazons*. It is used in Old Norse texts for such figures who were considered to have existed in eastern and central Europe. So, the idea leaped from the Russian usage to an Old Norse cliché for warrior women. Jesch comes to this conclusion by examining the Old Norse text passages that use the term and exposing the links to this Russian origin.

This, she points out, does not mean that there were no Viking women who fought. Rather, she suggests that the term *shield-maiden* be avoided and the more neutral terminology such as *female warrior* or similar be used.

Jesch specifically says that while the existence of the term *shield-maiden* does not prove the existence of real female warriors, neither does her analysis of the word rebut the possibility of real female warriors in the Viking Age:

> There is no doubt that human beings are capable of most things, and it cannot be denied that the existence of female warriors or military leaders in the Viking Age remains a possibility. Indeed I have always acknowledged this possibility even though I have also urged that the strongly binary emphasis on gender distinctions in a variety of evidence from the Viking Age itself means that it remains unlikely.

ARTS AND CRAFTS OF THE VIKING AGE

Artists and craftspeople of the Viking Age created images of armed female figures.

Hårby

One famous metal female figurine from the ninth century from Hårby in Denmark is armed with a sword and a shield. It could be a Valkyrie, a human shield-maiden, or a human woman defending her home.

Gilded silver figurine dated to the ninth century, 1.3 inches tall, found by a metal detector in 2012 at Hårby in Denmark. *National Museum of Denmark, Wikimedia Commons*

Hedeby

In another Viking figure, from Hedeby, Germany, one female appears on horseback and with a lance, while another stands before the horse holding a shield.

Two-character figure, one on horseback. A Viking Age gilded silver mount (silver covered in a thin layer of gold) from the manor at Tissø on Sjælland, Denmark. *National Museum of Denmark*

The person atop the horse wears the knotted hairstyle of a woman but also wears trousers, which were seen typically on men. The person in front of the horse wears a gown, has a female hair knot, carries a shield, and wears a helmet. There is nothing to suggest they are anything other than real women, but virtually all researchers have characterized them as Valkyrie figures. Some say that the horse is saddleless, like the horses the Valkyries rode off on at the end of the "Song of Spears."

Art that is dated to the Viking Age is actual and contemporaneous Viking thought, unlike the sagas written several hundred years later. Since these artworks were actually created by Viking people, are they better or more weighty evidence of real female warriors? Perhaps. But like art today—or of any time period—it is not necessarily a representation of a fact. It too can be interpretive and fictional.

WRITTEN HISTORICAL RECORDS

The people the Vikings encountered had a few things to say about it. Their viewpoint may have colored the events for any number of reasons. Some of the medieval monks described the pagan Vikings as noble and misguided. Others viewed their raids as the devil's work. Still other victims believed the raids were punishment from God for their own sins.

Many English leaders believed that the Christian God was somehow directing or influencing the Viking attacks as punishment. In 1009, after an intense Viking attack, King Æthelred issued a law with a program of fasting, almsgiving, and prayer so that the people could obtain God's mercy and gain his help in withstanding this enemy.

Dead Female Viking Warriors on a Battlefield in 971

In one account from military campaign records, John Skylitzes records the presence of dead female Viking warriors on a battlefield. They were found by people who were looting the scene of a raid in the year 971, in Bulgaria. They described turning over one body after another and seeing women "equipped like men."

The Red Girl in the Mid-Tenth Century

The province of Munster, Ireland, in the mid-tenth century was attacked by no fewer than sixteen raiding flotillas of Vikings. The event was recorded with such detail that the fleets were all written down with their commanders' names. The last entry was labeled "the fleet of the Inghen Ruiadh." This translates as the "Red Girl" or "Red Daughter," and was taken to refer to her hair color. Some experts who have considered the entries have interpreted her as the ship's captain and fleet commander.

Historical military records are mostly impressions of those who wrote them, which would tend to make them "fresh" recollections rather than a look back. However, the two referenced above were not written down later than the tenth century. The writings are not by Vikings; they are by the victims. Could the writers have colored the recitations for their own purposes, and if so, what purpose might that be? They can be distinguished from the sagas in that they are not presented as stories or fiction. Or not?

Other Graves and Other Bones

Birka's Bj 581 is not the only female Viking grave with weapons. Others exist and have been osteologically and archaeologically validated but not yet DNA tested.

- **Asnes, Norway:** In 1900, a large grave mound was excavated on a farm at Asnes, in Hedmark County, in Norway. In it a skeleton lay with a double-edged sword by the left side, its hilt by the hip and the point near the head. An ax, a spearhead, a shield boss, five arrowheads, a bent lancehead, a whetstone, and an iron file were arranged around the body. At the foot of the grave lay a bridled horse. The grave was dated to the mid-900s, similar to Bj 581.

  At first the grave was thought to belong to a man because of the weapons, but upon osteological examination, the remains were agreed to be of an eighteen-to-nineteen-year-old woman of a height of about five foot one and weight of approximately eighty-eight pounds. Archaeologists have had many varied opinions about this woman and her grave goods.

• **Aunvollen, Norway:** In an unmarked grave in Aunvollen, near Snåsavattnet in Nord-Trøndelag, Norway, a person who was osteologically determined to be female was found laid on a bed of textiles and down feathers, possibly a comforter. Next to her was a scabbarded sword, sickle, eight gaming pieces, a quartzite stone, whetstone, comb, scissors, 120 iron fragments (mostly of nails and rivets), and a spearhead.

• **Grave BB, Bogøvej, Island of Langeland, Denmark:** The grave of a woman in a Viking cemetery was found among forty-nine others who were excavated by archaeologists in the 1980s on the island of Langeland in Denmark. Grave BB was a secluded wooden chamber grave. The grave contained a woman who died between the age of sixteen and eighteen. She was lying on her back and her arms were extended. On her chest lay a knife, on her pelvis was an Arabic silver coin that dated to the tenth century, and at her right knee was positioned an ax. The ax did not appear to be a domestic tool. Its weight and shape were typical of a battle-ax that was made for killing. A replica of the ax was constructed by a weapons specialist and it was tested as if in combat on a pig's carcass, which is similar to the human form in that it resembles the same flesh and bone composition and comparative resistance. A small-framed woman testing the replica easily wielded deadly blows with the weapon.

Archaeologists have excavated many additional women's graves containing weapons. The types of weapons include swords, spears, miniature spears, shields, miniature shields, bows and arrows, horses, and riding equipment. Interpreting these weapons is complex and covers uses from household to farming, from folklore to medical to magic and spiritual.

These female Viking graves with weapons are real archaeological finds. Their female sex designations were made by osteologists, but they all await DNA testing for absolute confirmation.

Do they add to the weight of evidence that there were female Viking warriors? Would they be more valuable as evidence if the DNA testing confirmed they were women? If the DNA testing confirmed they were women, would there still be skeptics? And if everyone agreed they were female Viking warriors, what would they be like if you met them?

9

THE VIKING PHENOMENON AND THE TEAM'S FORMAL RESPONSE

THE TEAM TOOK A DEEP BREATH. The researchers would have pre-ferred that all their critics follow the classic approach of writing peer-reviewed papers, but that wasn't how it all came down. Most of the comments were emblazoned across the Internet.

The authors didn't wholesale reject all the criticisms, but they weren't about to jump into the endless social media churn. They'd already planned a second paper, and it seemed even more necessary now—to answer what they thought were flatly wrong assertions.

Neil Price took the lead on the second paper. He is well known for his expert knowledge of the Vikings and trying to get inside the Viking mind.

DR. NEIL PRICE: ARCHAEOLOGIST, PROFESSOR, AND VIKING AGE EXPERT

Neil Price's family went to a lot of museums while he was grow-ing up, but the one that really captured his attention was the British Museum. From the first time he went there, he couldn't get enough of archaeology, and at seventeen, he volunteered as a digger at the Museum of London. This gave him the amazing chance to participate in the excavation of Roman and medieval

Neil Price. *Courtesy of Neil Price*

archaeological sites. But it was the Vikings who really piqued his curiosity.

In 1985, Price dove into Viking studies earnestly. He earned a BA in medieval archaeology in 1988, at University College London's Institute of Archaeology. Then he did postgraduate research at the University of York, where he researched the artifacts from the Viking dig at Coppergate in York, UK. He even dug at Birka in 1990.

Price next joined the faculty at Uppsala University in Sweden and, at the same time, became a consulting professor for Harvard University in the United States. He followed this with achieving his PhD at Uppsala in 2002.

He has authored several books. *The Viking Way* has been called one of the most important contributions to Viking studies in recent years, and *Children of Ash and Elm* is said to be the history that presents Vikings on their own terms.

In 2015, Price became the director of the Viking Phenomenon Project (VPP), a center of excellence for the study of the Viking Age.

The project's focus was to shed light on the muddled early history of the Vikings.

The VPP shunned the same old worn-out themes. Instead, it trained its lens on the beginnings of the culture and what made the Vikings who they were. What made them set out to expand their reach at that time? What is the Viking contribution to Scandinavian history? How should the Swedish people handle the problematic perceptions of Vikings in current society? And did men and women play distinct roles in Viking culture?

Joining Price in the core research group were Charlotte Hedenstierna-Jonson and John Ljungkvist, plus a number of other postdoctoral researchers and international scholars.

Professionals in the Swedish archaeological community know (or know of) each other. Price had known the members of the Atlas Project for years, including Hedenstierna-Jonson, who worked with both projects. He'd also been following the Bj 581 saga ever since Anna Kjellström's early work. It was a natural that DNA testing of Scandinavian Iron Age skeletons, including Bj 581, could be relevant to the Viking Phenomenon Project.

Price, who has a self-effacing, wry humor, admitted, "Rather embarrassingly, I was also the guy who said 'Wow' when she [Kjellström] announced the osteological sex determination at that seminar in Stockholm way back in 2011."

Like Hedenstierna-Jonson, Price wasn't surprised by the Bj 581 DNA result. He had been confident that Kjellström and her team knew their stuff. But he was shocked by the flood of attention. The initial, ongoing, and increasing volume of the responses surprised him. And the fierceness with which some people clung to their belief that Viking women couldn't be warriors astonished him. It wasn't even just about the idea of a Viking woman of war. He couldn't understand the people who were willing to grasp at straws in order to deny the science.

Price recalled, "Rather than asking, 'What might this mean?' or discussing it with us, so many people simply rejected the idea."

THE TEAM'S REACTION

The Atlas team now felt they needed to respond to some of the crazier assertions that were being made. Price, as lead author, and the rest of the team approached the article with an arsenal of facts and a massive amount of additional material. They started from scratch with a complete review of the Stolpe findings and interpretation, worked their way through the criticisms, and finished by addressing social and gender issues.

The article, "Viking Warrior Women? Reassessing Birka Chamber Grave Bj.581," went through peer review for the Cambridge University Press journal *Antiquity* and was published in volume 93, issue 367, approximately a year and a half after the first article, online on February 18, 2019. The supplemental material that accompanies it is sizable.

Stolpe's Warrior Assessment

First off, Price set out why the team agreed with Stolpe that Bj 581 was a high-status warrior then, and why it remains so now. He touched on every item in the grave and its surroundings:

- the town and culture of war and its garrison area
- the location, size, construction, and elevation of the grave
- the possible meanings of the horses
- the impressive array of weapons and their positioning in the grave
- the spear thrown over the body and its possible meaning
- the person's attire and its international connections
- the coins, vessels, buckles, straps, and belt set
- the probable game board and the gaming pieces that seem to have been in the person's lap.

Stolpe's Sex Assessment

It was undeniable that the DNA confirmed that the person was female. But could the team absolutely, positively prove that the person in the grave was a female *warrior*? No, the researchers said, they couldn't absolutely, positively prove it. However, they stood by their belief that it is the most likely interpretation. They firmly disagreed with Stolpe's "male" assumption.

According to Price, "It is important to remember that when Bj 581 was recorded, male biological sex was not only conflated with a man's gendered identity, but also that warriorhood was presumed to be an exclusively masculine pursuit; the same interpretation would undoubtedly have been made had no human bone survived at all."

Next, they ticked through the most common headline-grabbing criticisms.

The Scandal of the Mixed-Up Bones

As Kjellström had done before, Price and the team explained that not all the Birka boxes were a mess. The Bj 581 box was intact, and moreover, every bone was individually inked with the grave number. The box did have the one stray femur marked Bj 854, but that was an obviously misplaced bone (the possibility of which is why they're labeled individually).

In addition, the Bj 581–numbered bones matched Stolpe's drawing, and they *didn't* match the records of any other burial. Furthermore, all the osteologists examined the same bones independently, and they all said they were most likely female.

And finally, the DNA tests were done on the *same* bones, and the result was female, using a chromosomal definition of sex.

The Curious Case of the Multiple Bodies

Some of the team's frustrations were evident on this topic. They reminded their critics that first of all, in his 1879 report, Stolpe explicitly wrote that it contained a *single body*.

In Fedir Androshchuk's peer-reviewed article, he asserted Stolpe had somehow not considered a second male body to be associated with the original male grave because it was a later burial, apparently on top of, or close by, the Bj 581 chamber. The team appreciated that Androschuk took the time to write a peer-reviewed article, but they vigorously disagreed with his assertion.

According to Price,

> In short, there is nothing whatsoever in the original descriptions of the grave to suggest a double burial, which is why in the formal reports of the Birka excavations Bj 581was published as containing only one individual. ([Holger] Arbman 1943: 188–90, and [Anne-Sofie] Gräslund 1980: 37–39, 74–75) . . .
>
> The problem here is simple, in that both Arwidsson and Androshchuk read Vilkans' report as an inventory of the *actual grave assemblages* rather than the *contents of the storage boxes*: the two things are very different. When one examines the bones (as Arwidsson and Androshchuk did not) it becomes quickly apparent that the extra femur is labelled 'Bj. 854,' designating a different grave . . .
>
> In contrast to Bj.581, the integrity of Bj.854 was found by Kjellström to be deeply compromised. It is therefore not difficult to understand that a bone from Bj.854 found its way into the wrong box, the possibility of which is precisely why bones and artifacts are labelled in the first place. Bj.854 also dates from perhaps a century earlier than Bj 581, (Gråslund 1980:27) and ironically the size of the extra femur, suggests that it too comes from a female, or possibly a teenager of indeterminate sex. . .
>
> On the basis on an unprecedentedly detailed study of the Birka human bone assemblage and its relationship to the excavated graves, closely correlated with all extant documentation, there is no doubt that Bj.581 only contain a single human body.

To this day, Price is still asked about a second body in the BJ 581 grave.

I still sometimes get questions like, "But can you *prove* that there wasn't originally a second male body also in the chamber, which has since somehow disappeared?" I tell them, "No, we can't, but only in the same way that we can't prove there was never a second *female* body there either. Or three of them in a pile, or an ostrich, or anything else for which there is no evidence whatsoever." Another way of putting it is that our critics are saying, "I don't agree with your interpretation, so I'm going to invent some evidence that doesn't exist . . . the second body . . . but if it *did*, it would prove you wrong." This is not how science should be done. And as to the scientific method, not one of the critics came to the museum to examine the bones or compare them to Stolpe's materials.

The buried person has always carried two X chromosomes, even if this was unknown before our recent work; the occupant of Bj 581 will never be biologically male again.

Sex Versus Gender—You Can't Say the Person Identified as Female

According to the team (and just about everyone else), the sex of Bj 581 raises deeper questions about women, gender, and social norms. Most archaeologists will concede that gender has long been a problem in their field of study. The difference between sex and gender has overwhelmingly been blurred.

The team's response was frank: "Can we be sure that the female-bodied person in Bj 581 identified as a woman? No, we cannot. She may have taken on a man's social role, while retaining a feminine identity. Queer theory also provides a potentially fruitful means of engaging with this individual, and their sense of self may have been—in our terms—non-binary or gender-fluid; identity may have been something to negotiate, to choose and re-choose on a daily basis."

The Person May Have Been Transgender

A common observation made about the XX result was that the person might have been transgender. The team didn't outright reject the idea but questioned it. "While we understand this line of thinking in the context of contemporary social debates, it should be remembered that this is a modern politicized, intellectual and Western term, and as such, is problematic (some would say impossible) to apply to people of the remote past. There are many possibilities across a wide gender spectrum, some perhaps unknown to us, but familiar to the people of the time. We do not discount any of them."

Weapons Don't Always Mean War

It was a little like going in circles, but once the team had proven that the person was female, they had to readdress the question of whether this person was a warrior. How did they do that? Making comparisons was one way.

> Can we prove that the occupant of Bj. 581 was a warrior? This depends on definitions. We can first consider the non-literal interpretations. Perhaps she was a farmer, a housewife, a fisherwoman, a merchant, a craftworker, a poet, or a slave, buried with expensive and dangerous things that did not belong to her, and with none of her own possessions. Perhaps she was, for some reason, interred with objects that conferred a proxy identity that she never had when alive.
>
> Equally, she may have lived as a warrior, but in a symbolic sense. In this light, we should also consider other early medieval cemeteries, both in Scandinavia and beyond, where we find people buried with what were clearly non-functional weapons, either unfinished or in such poor repair as to be useless. Similarly, we find operational weapons interred with individuals such as young children, who could never have physically wielded them. . . .

What is important here, however, is that *all* these combinations of artefacts and individuals—whether preserved from life or bestowed after death—refer to the concept of bearing arms, the gendered notion of "warrior-ness." . . .

To be a warrior was, at least in part, a social construct, and not necessarily directly connected to entering actual combat. If such a thing applied to the person in Bj. 581, we do not know exactly how this operated, and it is possible that we are just seeing the high-end "straight-to-Valhöll" option from the Birka funeral directors, but it would have made this individual a warrior nonetheless.

It's All Wishful Thinking!

Many critics accused the team of feminist wishful thinking. Some of the sharpest claims were that they set out to produce a female Viking warrior. According to Kjellström, Hedenstierna-Jonson, and Price, the answer was emphatically *No!*

Kjellström explained that her assessment of Bj 581 was part of an overall population data gathering effort in the People in Transition in the Mälaren Valley project.

Hedenstierna-Jonson explained that the Atlas Project was a project to map the human genome of the Scandinavian people. She didn't put Bj 581 on the list for the purpose of trying to prove the person was female. She put the person's bones on the list to add the genome to the study and, given the disagreement between the assumptions by Stolpe and the osteologists, to find out once and for all which sex they were. That is a far cry from trying to prove a specific sex.

Price stated, "Were we interested? Of course. We're scientists. But one can't test DNA in such a way as to produce a desired result. It is what it is. We followed the trail of data and analysis. To those who attacked the 'high-ranking warrior' interpretation only after the person was shown to be female, I would ask why the interpretation wasn't a problem when the person in Bj 581 was believed to be male?"

THE CORE QUESTION: *ARE VIKING WARRIOR WOMEN FACT OR FICTION?*

According to the team, Bj 581 supports an interpretation that at least one Viking Age woman adopted a professional warrior lifestyle. And further, that it would be surprising if she was the only one. They also point to the presence of clothing and the gaming set that imply a position of command.

The unwillingness by some academics and scholars to entertain such an interpretation calls on all interested parties, according to Price, to question their assumptions. He calls them to ask questions such as:

What constitutes a weapon or a warrior, and how might we tell?

What links do we make between buried individuals and the items accompanying them?

What are our perceptions of gender and personal identity?

How do we extend what we know about such individuals to society in general?

"We must all be especially aware that such perceptions are ours and not necessarily those of Viking Age people," says Price. "In that light, we also need to examine ourselves as scholars—our own biases and prejudices—asking what we are prepared to find acceptable in the past, and why."

Is Bj 581 an exception to the norm that Viking warriors are mostly male? Price and the team agree that warriors were mostly male, but they argue:

"Currently, the figure of the woman with weapons seems to be an exception, but this does not mean that she can be deconstructed out of existence—especially on the basis of **Pavlovian skepticism**."

He and the rest of the team believe there may be more female Viking warriors, since most buried people during the Viking Age have been sexed without the use of DNA, but rather indirectly by using artifacts, material culture, and context. In fact, the team thinks it is more than possible that DNA will reveal additional female warriors.

But whether more can be predicted at this point or not, the relevance of Bj 581 cannot be ignored. It's important to archaeological studies of gender, violence, funerals, symbolism, and many other areas of study in general and the Viking Age.

"Which part of this person is (or is not) a 'fact'?" Price asks. "She adjusts and nuances our interpretations and challenges our stereotypes. She adds still further dimensions to our understanding of the Viking Age at a time of critical cultural transformation and social encounter."

But at the same time, Price resisted the idea that the Bj 581 grave should be made to bear the burden of all expectations or goals, whether they were consistent with or in opposition to the team's conclusions.

> Instead, this is a case study that, in some ways, presents more questions than answers but which also opens up previously unexpected possibilities. We as scholars—all of us in the multiple disciplines—stand before the collective corpus of excavated Viking Age burials with the task of patient and careful reassessment, in relation to not only gender but also concerning the social signals encoded within every aspect of funerary ritual.
>
> In the specific case of Bj 581, of course, one may draw different conclusions, but the integrity of the grave and the biological sex determination are secure. It is now for others to decide how they deal with the wider implications.

REACTIONS TO THE 2019 BJ 581 ARTICLE

The publication of the 2019 article started a new round of reactions, and interest in the team's work percolated. Much of the chatter was again online, but one source of commentary deserved attention.

In his 2021 book, *Women and Weapons in the Viking World: Amazons of the North,* Leszek Gardeła, archaeologist, postdoctoral researcher at the National Museum of Denmark, and specialist in Viking women and weapons, wrote an extensive analysis of the Bj 581 grave and the reaction to the team's second article.

Leszek Gardeła. *Courtesy of Mira Fricke*

Gardeła was persuaded that the bones doubtlessly belong to grave Bj 581. He noted that they were clearly labeled with ink and that there was no reason to think that they had been mixed up.

For him, the claim that Bj 581 included two individuals had thus been rejected and that Price and the team had demonstrated that the additional femur bone in one of the boxes labeled Bj 854 belonged to a female individual or a teenager of indeterminate sex, from another grave. So, starting from the premise that the team had maintained the initial argument from 2017 and expressed the opinion that Bj 581 *is* the grave of a female warrior, he point-by-point addressed what he thought were inconsistencies to be considered.

"If Charlotte Hedenstierna-Jonson, Neil Price and their team are right in their assumptions that Bj. 581 was actually a single grave of a biological woman—and indeed their 2019 study is very convincing in that regard—we must still remain open to alternate interpretations."

—Leszek Gardeła

Highlights of Gardeła's observations include:

- Stolpe wasn't always present at the site and sometimes he made his notes on the finds after they had been excavated by his workers. This creates the possibility that some things were lost in translation.

- The dynamite used to remove the boulder may have damaged the grave's contents.

- Chamber graves were not open and shut only once. The grave could be entered and visited after the funeral. This could have affected the contents of the grave by the addition, removal, and even destruction of objects and bodies.

"Grave disturbance was commonly practiced in the Viking world, including the cemeteries at Birka. . . . These acts were not always intended to gain material wealth: sometimes graves were accessed to establish supernatural contact with the deceased, to obtain special or 'enchanted' objects (e.g. family heirlooms), to perform magic or to maim or annihilate the dead."

—Gardeła

- Swords in graves were typically placed on the right-hand side of the body. This was true in the majority of Birka graves, but not in Bj 581, Bj 850, and Bj 977. In these three graves, the swords were placed on the left-hand side of the deceased person. There are also two potentially female weapon graves from Norway where the swords were on the left side of the bodies. Gardeła asks whether left-side placement could have signaled something peculiar about these weapons and/or the identity of the dead. Or was this how swords in the Viking world were "supposed" to be buried with women? (Further complicating matters, a forensic scan of the Bj 581 bones commissioned by National Geographic suggested that the individual in Bj 581 was left-handed.)

- The two shields and two spears do not necessarily indicate that there was a second body in the grave. However, even if there were two bodies, the two shields and spears could indicate that both persons were of similar status and both were buried like a warrior.

  As to the spears, one was located at the foot end of the grave pointing toward the platform with the two horses. This position might indicate that the spear had been thrust into the grave as part of a special ritual to dedicate the deceased person to Óðinn. Archaeologist Andreas Nordberg has suggested that the acts of thrusting weapons into graves might suggest the people buried in such graves might not have died in battle and their mourn-ers might have wanted to do something that would ensure they reached Valhalla. Support exists for this idea in Snorri Sturluson's Ynglinga saga where Óðinn is marked with a spear before he dies.

- Gaming pieces. The presence of gaming pieces and gaming boards in Viking archaeology and Old Norse literature is varied. Games have been found with males and females from different social classes and are not necessarily indicators of military rank. In addition, Old Norse literature reveals that playing strategy games, such as *hnefatafl*, was not a strictly male activity—several women from different social strata are portrayed as actively engaging in this pastime.

"We have to acknowledge the fact that board games and gaming pieces are not at all uncommon

in Viking Age funerary contexts, both in Scandinavia and in other parts of the Viking **diaspora**. . . . We
will never know for certain what exactly they meant
to the deceased person from Bj 581 and to those
who orchestrated the burial, but we should certainly
remain open to several alternative interpretations,
rather than arguing that they were just symbols of
rank in a martial environment."

—Gardeła

- The copper alloy bowl: These bowls are usually found in high-status graves and most often placed at the feet of the deceased. Some are plain, as the one in the Bj 581 grave is, but some have flowers, animals, and geometric designs. Sometimes bowls are associated with Christian rituals, but given the evidence of pagan acts like burying seated and the thrust of the spear, it is more likely the bowl was a prized possession of the deceased or placed there by mourners with a special intention in mind.

  Gardeła notes that copper alloy bowls have been associated predominantly with burials of men. In view of this, the presence of the bowl in Bj 581 can be seen as indication of the ambiguous identity of the grave's occupant.

- Riding equipment: Usually, Viking graves that contain stirrups also contain spurs, but in Bj 581 there were no spurs. The lack of spurs, which would have formed a standard set used by heavily equestrian warriors, might be explained in at least two ways. According to Gardeła, they might have been removed from the grave at some point after the burial ceremony, or the person buried in the grave preferred an Eastern, nomadic style of riding in which case the spurs would have been unnecessary.

> "Together with the rare silver hat cap (with parallels in Kievan Rus), the lack of spurs amplifies the idea that the deceased person (and/or those who conducted the burial) had strong eastern connections."
>
> —Gardeła

- Trauma to the bones: Some have made much of the lack of scars and other trauma to the bones. Gardeła thinks this should be taken with a grain of salt and should not be used as a decisive argument for or against their warrior status. He and other archaeologists agree that the life of a Viking warrior, similar to the life of any warrior, did not have to involve engaging in actual physical combat and did not have to end in a violent way on the battlefield. It is obvious that weapons in the Viking Age were created with the intention to make them effective in combat, but it is impossible to know whether every person who owned a weapon actually had the opportunity to use it on the battlefield.

- Gardeła's overall observations. Gardeła concludes that grave Bj 581 is exceptional in all sorts of ways, that it can be approached from many different angles, and that Price, Hedenstierna-Jonson, and the team have made a convincing argument. Yet he cautions, "[W]e must still remain open to alternative interpretations. In view of the ongoing debate surrounding weapon graves in early medieval Europe, some scholars will certainly remain skeptical of the idea all people buried with weapons—including the occupant of Bj 581—actively participated in warfare or broadly-understood martial activities."

Gardeła's assessment is one of the most in depth and broad rang-
ing. It validates many core aspects of the team's interpretation, challenges others, and raises new issues for consideration. He points to
Old Norse literature to emphasize and support his interpretations.
Overall, his analysis highlights the unique relationship of different
experts and how they contribute to Viking studies.

But where does Gardeła come down on whether the person in
Bj 581 is a warrior?

Well, he can't confirm that. But, on the other hand, neither does
he think it is impossible or wishful thinking that she was. According
to Gardeła, "It is quite possible that she was."

10

FACE-TO-FACE WITH
A BIRKA WARRIOR

UNTIL THE 1970S, Viking archaeology focused on tangible grave goods: weapons, textiles, coins, and jewelry. These items were generally viewed as reflecting sex. Weapons meant men, and jewelry meant women. Further, an ax in a male grave meant an implement of war, while an ax in a female grave was construed as a tool. This is referred to as *gendering artifacts*. Once the grave goods suggested a sex, there was less focus on the people in the graves as individuals.

Increasingly, prominent archaeologists have challenged this practice, and focus has been turned to the individuals. Today, topics such as "the Viking mind," "how Vikings saw themselves," and "Viking Age gender fluidity" have become subjects of intense study. In the case of a few graves, like Bj 581, the scrutiny has been so intense it could be said these individuals have been awakened. They have started to become real people.

In addition, osteology, chemical testing, genomic testing, and other modern technologies have allowed reasonable estimations of height, weight, age, birthplace, travels, and in some cases the modeling of features. The interplay of these physical qualities with grave goods, sagas, poetry, and other artifacts of the Viking Age has inspired visual interpretations of Viking people.

But still, as archaeologist Martin Rundkvist wrote in 2017 regarding Bj 581, "Your skeleton can't tell us anything about your gender, and your grave goods can't tell us anything about your osteo-sex [the sex of your bones]."

Research is advancing quickly in this field, and some information presented here might already be surpassed by newer understandings. In addition, not everyone is of the same mind as to gender basics across the medical and nonmedical spectrum. For the purpose of the Bj 581 discussion that follows, here are some understandings, as of 2022.

Chromosomes are representative of sex, not gender. Sex and gender are often confused. They are not the same thing, and they are not interchangeable. Furthermore, gender is not binary (either female or male), and neither is sex. Sex is biology, while gender is culture. Physiological traits do not always correlate with chromosomes. Beyond that, understandings and interpretations of sex and gender can vary among and within societies.

- **Karyotypes determine sex.** It is generally accepted that sex is determined by karyotype. Karyotype is a person's collection of forty-six chromosomes (in most cases forty-four autosomes plus two sex chromosomes) in the nuclei of their cells. Karyotypes have been documented to include: X, XX, XXY, XY, XYY, and XXXY. Some of these are genetic variations with extra copies of the X or Y chromosome in each of their cells. XX is the most common female, and XY is the most common male. But there are some people who are not simply male or female. Some people have XY karyotypes but female sex organs. Others have XX karyotypes and male sex organs.

- **Cisgender** describes a person whose gender identity and sex assigned at birth correspond in a traditional sense (e.g., a man assigned a male sex at birth).

- **Transgender** is defined by the LGBTQ and Allies at Harvard

Medical School as "an umbrella term for people whose gender identity does not align with the traditional expectations of the sex they were assigned at birth." A transgender woman would be a woman whose sex at birth was assigned as male. A transgender man would be a man whose sex at birth was assigned as female.

- **Gender identity** is a phrase that is used to describe the core of a person's self-perceived gender. It's how people feel about themselves and how they present themselves to others.

- **Gender expression** is often used to describe cultural behaviors such as dress and mannerisms that differentiate people in the masculine/feminine spectrum. All humans engage in gender expression, which is defined by the Harvard Medical School: Sexual and Gender Minority Health Equity Initiative as "how someone communicates their gender through clothing, hairstyle and grooming, body language, behavior, and other aspects of outwardly displaying gender."

- **Intersex**, sometimes called "differences in sex development," is the term that describes "diversity in sex characteristics whereby reproductive organs, genitals, or other sexual anatomy differ from traditional expectations for female or male." According to Dr. Patricio Gargollo of the Mayo Clinic, "Each year a portion of the population is born with biological characteristics— sex chromosomes, gonads, genitalia, hormones, or a combination—that don't align with textbook definitions of male or female. The most common of such intersex traits is *congenital adrenal hyperplasia* and occurs as a result of prenatal overexposure of male hormones (androgens). Some differences are noticed at birth and sometimes not until puberty or later." Some people with intersex traits live their entire lives unaware they have a difference between their chromosomes and their physical appearance. This is not the same as transgender.

So, what was the gender of the person in grave Bj 581?

Faced with the XX DNA results, the grave goods (which were primarily weapons), and the relevant literature and texts, experts have ventured to imagine a gender impression for this individual.

The Birka Museum experts, in conjunction with the museum's 2021–2022 Birka exhibit, *Buried at Birka: Three Centuries, Four Viking Lives*, took the step to create human images of the skeletons in four Viking graves. They replicated the grave goods, including clothing and weapons, and dressed and equipped live models of similar body characteristics with these items.

Applying the interpretation of Hedenstierna-Jonson and Price and their team, the museum brought the person in Bj 581 to life in a vivid red tunic and her cap with its multitude of small mirrors.

This isn't the first time someone has made an effort to imagine the physical person buried in Bj 581. In 2001, Tancredi Valeri drew his version of what the warrior may have looked like, using clothing details recorded in research of various Birka chamber burials and graves of the same period from Moshchevaya Balka in the North Caucasus.

Thus, the bones of the person in Bj 581 have gone from their resting place in a chamber grave under a boulder, to Stolpe's illustrations, to refined drawings of Stolpe's illustrations, to osteological morphological examination, to DNA processing, to monochromatic figure illustration, and to full-color photographs of a living human depicting a female Viking warrior.

There are challenges associated with stepping into the academic spotlight with a visual gender interpretation of a one-thousand-year-old person. Whether it's a work of fiction, a piece of art, or a video game, it's going to be either correct or it's not, and there is no way of knowing which it is. It's going to be embraced by some and rejected—even vilified—by others.

Scholarly expertise, reasonableness, and good old-fashioned facts provide the basis for interpretation. Price readily offers that the team can't absolutely know where this person was on the gender spectrum. They could be wrong in their interpretation of her as a

Tancredi Valeri illustration based on the Birka chamber records and on the graves from Moshchevaya Balka in the North Caucasus of the same period. © *Neil Price. Courtesy of Neil Price.*

cisgender woman. However, they see this as most likely based on the facts they have.

Critics of their interpretation agree that it's impossible to know how the Bj 581 occupant presented from a gender perspective. But almost to a person, they also agree that if there was only one body in grave Bj 581, the bones tested belonged to that body, and the weapons were associated with those bones, then it is, of course, possible that the person was a female Viking warrior.

GENDER ARCHAEOLOGY

A subfield of archaeological study emerged in the 1970s that questioned the approach of labeling items as being male or female and following that with a strict male or female sex determination. The field is referred to as *gender archaeology.*

The topics of sex and gender weren't entirely new to Viking Age studies. In fact, before the 1970s there had been a great deal of research on gender roles as they existed during the Viking Age. The problem is that the research tended to reinforce what is called *cultural bias.* To have a cultural bias is to consciously or unconsciously judge another culture by the values and standards of one's own culture. For example, if an archaeologist comes from a culture where only men build fires, then her cultural bias might be that a one-thousand-year-old firepit was naturally used by a man.

In the book *Exploring Sex and Gender in Bioarchaeology*, the authors examine the ways in which cultural biases creep into research. It can be seen in the questions archaeologists ask (and do not ask) when interpreting data. Specifically, they show how long-held beliefs about sex and gender can distort understanding of a society and obscure events of the past.

According to gender archaeologist Marianne Moen, "A knife is an object, a material truth that cannot be denied. But it ceases to be an object in this sense as soon as it enters an interpretation of what it means, and then it becomes something else, something imbued with modern ideas about past uses, as well as the object itself. Thus, archaeological knowledge is produced knowledge, and produced knowledge exists within a historical context which needs to be acknowledged."

Moen has also noted that the publication of the Bj 581 research has increased scholarly attention to gender archaeology. She and others have been intrigued by the notion of exploring social roles across the Viking population rather than within traditionally gendered categories that are based on grave goods.

"The Dead Don't Bury Themselves"

As is it often said by archaeologists, "The dead don't bury themselves." For the purpose of knowledge, archaeologists work with artifacts and settings that the deceased may not have selected or arranged. Thus when a grave is excavated, there is more to be learned about the person who was buried in it than their stature, physique, sex, or manner of death. It is the living who ultimately select the site, treat and position the body, and choose animals that may accompany the deceased, as well as other grave goods. Survivors even provide for rights of visitation inside tombs and chamber graves. These choices made by the living are believed to be appropriate representations relative to the life of the dead person, although they may, in some cases, seek to enlarge their reputations. For example, relatives may seek to make a person appear loftier than they were in life. Archaeologists examine burials with such a possibility in mind.

The gist of the discussion has been to challenge the idea that violence and war were only man's work and household activities were only in the woman's domain. Moen and others urge that in questioning these ideas, the possibility of a *gender-fluid* Viking Age society will emerge. But what exactly does that mean? It does not mean proving that females were involved in combat or that men cooked but rather the idea that gender characteristics are on a spectrum or range rather than opposites in absolute categories. It could also mean that a person's gender expression could vary by age, activity, day, location, and numerous other factors.

By necessity, over decades of digs and the gathering of artifacts, classifications have evolved. It is in this process that some of the misconceptions have developed. Moen points specifically to Viking

Age keys. Keys were interpreted as used by the woman of the house. This reinforced that keys in a grave meant a female burial. Other analysis, however, has shown that keys were as frequent in male graves as female graves. Another example is scales. In a female grave, scales were considered a household item, yet in a male grave they were deemed to show work in a trade. These two examples illustrate how interpretations were not based on the objects, since they were the same in all graves.

Herein lies the problem of associating grave goods with social roles. Does a scale in a grave indicate a man and also that the man was involved in trade? Perhaps. But why does that same analysis not apply to female graves? The grave goods could also have been gifts, could symbolize an ideal rather than a real situation, could have been bribes to the dead to keep them from returning, and more. Yet, according to Moen, grave goods are still a principal source for interpretation of identity.

A gender archaeology approach does not deny the physical differences between men and women, but it questions the idea that these differences determine personality, potential, and characteristics. Until the availability of DNA testing, osteology was the only scientific method of testing sex. Both methods, however, depend on suitable bone or tooth material, and as was seen in the Bj 581 example, osteologist Berit Vilkans's morphological interpretation didn't rise to the prominence of the impression given by the grave goods.

The big concern is what to do with conflicting data and artifacts. What should be the primary gender indicator, if there are gender indicators at all? Moen contends that "gender is of secondary importance and that the wrong questions are being asked."

To facilitate the "gender fluid" discussion, Moen compiled data from 218 Viking burials from Norway with gender representations from traditional categories. The results showed both gender differences and gender similarities. But the large number of shared items defied the standard gender classifications.

Weapons were found in male graves *and* female graves. In addition, jewelry, which was found often in female graves, was found in 40 percent of the male graves. Categories that were considered less gendered, including cooking equipment, domestic animals, chests, keys, and other items associated with household matters, also revealed interesting patterns in their appearance in male versus female graves.

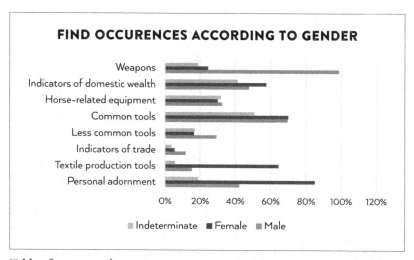

Table of grave goods. © *Moen 2019*

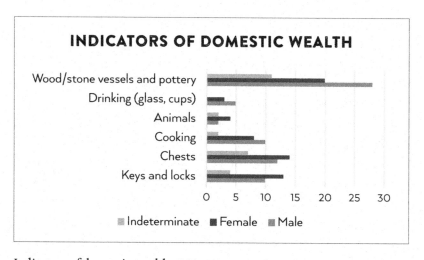

Indicators of domestic wealth. © *Moen 2019*

Moen suggests that the traditional gender divide imagined in the Viking Age may be artificial. Furthermore, she notes that there are many burials that cannot be assigned a gender.

> If gendered graves are used for interpretations of gender roles, the graves that do not display a clear gender affiliation must also be allowed to be equally representative. Researchers cannot allow them to be discounted because of what they lack, as it is modern perceptions that interpret them as incomplete in comparison with other burials.

Moen goes on to observe that almost a quarter of the graves do not comply with the traditional male/female compartments in the Viking Age and that researchers should look outside the narrow categories. She urges that perhaps the gender classifications are not as "supremely important" as has been assumed.

Moen observes that the presence and display of weapons in the graves was viewed differently for males. Male-gendered burials often contained multiple weapons, whereas fourteen of seventy-three female graves contained axes, five contained arrowheads, two contained a spearhead, and at least one contained a shield boss. Her point was that war and violence, while pervasive in the Viking Age, is not gender exclusive, nor does it exclude common and parallel uses of weapons. So, in short, while carrying a weapon may indicate social status, it need not signify only maleness.

References to women as natural caregivers and men as natural hunters and doers can be seen in **Charles Darwin**'s writings, which contributed to the upper-class Victorian ideas and culture he lived in. Here may lie the source of many of the gendered assumptions made in academic fields to this day. Though these assumptions preceded Darwin, he was hugely influential, and it is important to recognize that his assumptions about gender were shaped by his scientific and cultural context in the late 1880s and they cannot be blindly applied to the Viking Age.

Moen observes that although it may be difficult to finely describe an ideal for Viking Age females, it certainly would not have anything in common with Victorian feminine ideals. This emphasizes the problem of applying modern thought to the past. The actual remains do not support the assumptions that Viking women would not have been involved in or committed to the war efforts of their community.

Last, she says that modern prejudices must be abandoned if we are going to ask meaningful questions about the identity in the Viking Age.

> These include fixed beliefs that gender is biologically determined as binary (either/or) male or female. . . . If researchers are to truly approach the question of what an ideology of war may have looked like, they first need to decide how they define social ideologies. . . . It would be naïve to think that only one half of the population was invested in it.

CHECKING YOUR BIAS

Archaeologists will tell you it is a monumental task to self-examine, or "check your bias," when doing research. When looking at anything past or present, humans are not easily separated from their ingrained beliefs and opinions. That being the case, it is difficult to exercise objectivity in research and reaching conclusions.

When it comes to gender, objectivity is even more challenging. It's affected by family, politics, religion, relationships, education, biology, and sometimes finger-pointing, calling out, name-calling, and canceling. But in the end, interpretations are nothing more than interpretations.

The goal, scholars urge, is to have an objective baseline of understanding to start from. This doesn't mean there can't be competing theories on what is objective. Just as archaeologists inventory what is found in a grave, they may also comment on what is curiously *not* there.

Bioarchaeologist Rebecca Gowland warned of the gender stereotypes that take hold in interpreting graves such as with Bj 581. A professor of archaeology at Durham University, Gowland suggested what she considered the obvious: the Bj 581 grave had particularly rich military commander history until it was identified as a woman, and then it was somehow no longer a warrior. Further, when female osteologists correctly tried to report that the skeleton was female, they were ignored. She urged that we must allow the space for women to be buried with weapons and men to be buried with jewelry.

"We need to start thinking about [gender roles] as a bit more fluid and less strict and stop talking about men and women in different ways when they are buried the same way."

—Marianne Moen

WOMEN AND WAR

Despite the sensational news coverage of Bj 581, people other than cisgender men have fought in wars.

Women Cross-Dressed to Join the Army and Navy in the Netherlands

In *The Tradition of Female Transvestism in Early Modern Europe* by Rudolf M. Dekker and Lotte C. van de Pol, the authors describe women in the Netherlands who dressed as men and joined the army and navy between 1550 and 1839. Their research took them into the world of ballads and folktales and raised questions about the overlap between social reality and literature or myth—not unlike how Viking Age scholars do research using both artifacts and sagas. Similarly, their results raised questions about how people construct a social identity.

Women Were Soldiers at Waterloo

Women were found on the field at Waterloo dressed as soldiers. On June 18, 1815, during a calm between skirmishes, British troops found two dead Frenchwomen. "I saw one of them," recounted Captain Henry Ross-Lewin of the 32nd Regiment of Foot. "She was dressed in a nankeen jacket and trousers, and had been killed by a ball which had passed through her head."

Women and Transgender Men Fought in the American Civil War

Both the Union and Confederate armies would not allow women to enlist, but an estimated four hundred women managed to get in anyway by disguising themselves. Many of the recruits were young men whose faces were smooth and chins were beardless, so women were less noticeable among them. In addition, there was such a dire need for troops that medical requirements were slim. If a recruit had basic body parts and could hold a musket, that was considered good enough. So, with dirt on their faces, loose clothing, and short hair, the women passed muster.

Stories About Amazon Women Have Been Told for Centuries

Another group of militaristic women, the so-called Amazons, have appeared in history in one century then another, on one continent and then another, but for the most part have been accepted as fictional characters. That is, except for the well-documented women warriors of the eighteenth and nineteenth century West African kingdom of Dahomey (in today's Benin). These are women who were taught to fight, to handle weapons, to be strong, and to withstand suffering. They hunted and had musical skills, but their basic purpose was to make war. It is reported that they lusted for battle, rushed into it with bloodcurdling cries, and fought with fury and valor. Their main weapons were muskets, clubs, and machetes. They were pitiless in victory and had a reputation for terrifying their neighbors.

Joan of Arc Fought as Joan

Then there was Joan of Arc, who fought as a woman in men's fighting gear. Joan is the French heroine who fought during the Hundred Years' War and was canonized as a saint. Ultimately, she was placed at the head of the French army where the troops accepted her direction and advice because they believed she was instructed by God. Despite an incidence of traveling dressed as a male soldier for safety (and being accused of cross-dressing), she led her life as a female and was always known to be a woman. She jumped from a seventy-foot tower to escape her imprisonment and engaged in other acts of risk and bravery. Her life was marked by her fight for religion, not by her sex.

General Casimir Pulaski May Have Been Intersex

And there was General Casimir Pulaski, war hero of the American Revolution. In the 1990s, forensic anthropologists exhumed the remains of General Washington's renowned founder of the

Casimir Pulaski
portrait by Jan Skyka.
Wikimedia Commons

American cavalry. When they examined the bones, they immediately concluded they were those of a female. The skeleton underwent more than eight years of examination that showed it to be consistent with Pulaski's age and military service, including a defect on the right cheekbone and a healed wound on the skull that was consistent with historical records of an injury he received. Everyone agreed that he was a person of small stature, but despite his size he was reputed to be a powerful and skilled fighter who was light and nimble on horseback. He was also known for his privacy and avoidance of intimate relationships.

Two rounds of DNA testing ultimately resolved, to a high degree of probability, the identity of the bones as being Pulaski's. The most recent study funded by the Smithsonian Institution were released in 2019. The study cited a number of typically female features and referred to a hypothesis that Pulaski may have been female or intersex.

Recent Studies Have Identified the Body of a Person in Finland Who Had XXY Chromosomes

A Viking grave excavated in 1968 in Suontaka Vesitorninmäki, Hattula, Finland, uncovered a person whom many archaeologists interpreted as female because of the presence of traditionally female clothing and jewelry. In addition, one sword was found on the left side and another on the right side of the person. This caused other archaeologists to deny the female interpretation and/or conclude it must have been a double burial. It was unclear whether the swords were in the original burial, but nonetheless, the grave has been held up by many an example of a powerful woman.

In 2021, a paper published in the *European Journal of Archaeology* described how scientists examined a body that was anatomically male, but when they DNA tested it, the chromosomes were XXY. This chromosomal configuration is known as *Klinefelter's syndrome*. In this syndrome, a male has an extra X chromosome (i.e., XXY chromosomes). The researchers wrote, "The individual could have been a respected member of a community because of their physical and psychological differences from the other members of that community; but it is also possible that the individual was accepted as a non-binary person because they already had a distinctive or secured position in the community for other reasons; for example, by belonging to a relatively wealthy and well-connected family."

Women in the Armed Forces Today

The ban on women in combat in the US armed forces was eliminated in 2015. Since that time, the number of women seeking combat positions has been rising steadily. They have earned positions of leadership in marine corps platoons, air force wings, combat vessels, howitzer section chiefs, and numerous army units. They also now serve in the infantry, field artillery, armor, cavalry, fire support, and special forces. There have been female fighter pilots and helicopter pilots, and the air force has more female generals than any other branch except the navy.

WERE VIKINGS GENDER RIGID, GENDER FLUID, GENDER BENDING . . . DOES IT MATTER?

The larger question remains of whether it really matters if the gender of Bj 581 is pinned down. More to the point, did it matter in Viking society? Does an examination of gender identity possibilities in Viking society help the interpretation of Bj 581? Does it also raise the topic of whether Viking society was "gender fluid" and "gender identity accepting"?

Price writes in *Children of Ash and Elm*,

> In a sense it does not really matter whether the person in the Birka grave was a female-bodied warrior woman or not (though as one of the lead authors in the research team, I firmly believe she was all those things). This person may equally have been transgender, in our terms, or non-binary, or gender fluid. There are other possibilities, too, but the point is that *they must all be recognized as possible Viking-Age identities* while—crucially—not assuming

this must be the case. Not least, in the interpretation of Bj 581, scholars should be careful not to deny the basic agency of women, and their potential to choose one way of life over others; this person does not have to be necessarily different. Furthermore, *all* these intersections of activity and identity were in themselves deeply gendered—from "warriorhood" to everything else. Importantly, none of this needed to be fixed and permanent. . . .

Up to a point, one should also resist the urge to categorize: perhaps Viking-Age people chose and renegotiated their identities every day, much as many of us do. Their ideas about gender went far beyond the binaries of biological sex, as scholars are now beginning to understand. Sadly, there has been much less awareness of the privilege required to grant ourselves such innocence for so long.

Price feels the Bj 581 grave has inadvertently shone a light on all the books and all the scholars who, for all these many generations, have been pretending that the Viking Age is an enormous monolith where everybody was the same, when all Viking people were clearly not. One of the things he finds so exciting about archaeology is that it demonstrates the difference. "Every time we excavate a grave it's a different person with different things. It's a different life."

Price points out that for centuries archaeologists have determined sex and gender through association with gendered objects and, "Beyond the obvious problems of conflating sex and gender, . . . these readings risk simply piling one set of assumptions on top of another in what forensic decision-makers call a 'bias snowball' of cumulatively questionable interpretations." He finds it unsatisfactory at best, and at worst it can lead to a potentially vast misreading of Viking Age gender from the literally tens of thousands of burials that have been analyzed in this way over the years.

But he doesn't think that all is lost. He believes that it all probably does reflect Viking Age reality—with a caveat.

Not *all* burials conform to such patterns, and an openness to the exceptions—which we know were there—is vital. Without this, one can never hope to do archaeological justice to the gender spectrum discernible in the medieval texts or compare this with Viking-Age empirical reality. More excitingly, the archaeology can turn up evidence for identities and genders that did not make it to the written sources.

So, does it really matter? Must we conclude that the person in the Birka grave was a female-bodied warrior woman or not? The researchers on the team firmly believe she was, and they have stated their reasons. But the person also may have been transgender, nonbinary, gender fluid, intersex, or some other classification that we have yet to identify.

Price often says when asked, "This is a grave with a biologically female occupant. What you think about that is up to you."

And when asked if she would like to meet the person in Bj 581 if she could, Charlotte Hedenstierna-Jonson replied, "If this woman actually was the warrior that she was buried as, she probably would have done not so very nice things, so she wouldn't have been a very good role model. She was a fierce person. So, I think not. Given the number of weapons in the grave, I'd settle for a view from a distance."

How about you? Would you like to meet the person who was buried in Bj 581?

ACKNOWLEDGMENTS

THIS BOOK BEGAN when I went to a lecture at the American Swedish Institute in Minneapolis, Minnesota, in 2019 and learned of the Bj 581 DNA results. As Charlotte Hedenstierna-Jonson showed slides of the grave and explained the history of the excavation and the century-later genomic project and Neil Price described the research and publication of results, I could hardly sit in my seat. I knew immediately that I wanted to tell young people about this incredible discovery. Before long, I learned of the academic disputes that arose out of the research, and I quickly realized the greater implications for gender discussions. A three-year deep dive into Viking studies and related research ensued.

My thanks to the archaeologists, historians, physicians, and geneticists who generously agreed to be interviewed and who helped me understand the complicated implications of this research, how scientific dialogue works, and how knowledge advances in this field. Particularly, I thank Charlotte Hedenstierna-Jonson, Anna Kjellström, Neil Price, Leszek Gardeła, Judith Jesch, Maja Krzewińska, Patricio Gargollo, as well as everyone who helped me in my research, including history research wizard Matthew Camp and translator Cindy Wentland.

My thanks to readers and reviewers who helped me shape the manuscript, find the narrative voice, and design the story arc—Robin Kirk, Kelly Dyksterhouse, Magda Surrisi, Anne Bowen, Jenn Barnes, Catherine Frank, Lynn Slaughter, Matthew Camp, and Vicki Palmquist.

And thank you to my wonderful agent Kelly Dyksterhouse, who believed in the project and found it a home.

Most of all, thank you to my editor Jerry Pohlen, who could see the deeper story in this "female Viking warrior" infatuation of mine. There is no greater gift to an author than an editor who shares your vision and can help you realize it. Thank you to publisher Cynthia Sherry for her support and enthusiasm for this book. And cheers to copyeditors Ben Krapohl, Cathy Jones, and Devon Freeny, who made sure every little detail was correct. Thanks to Jonathan Hahn, who designed the interior. And, of course, many thanks to the entire team at Chicago Review Press who applied their special editorial, design, marketing, and publicity skills to make this book a reality.

GLOSSARY

amber fossilized tree resin whose appealing natural beauty caused it to be traded for use in decorative objects and for folk medicine

archaeology the study of things that people have left behind

archaeologist researchers who excavate the places people have lived in order to find the things they have left behind

artifacts the things left behind

auricular surface the ear-shaped joint surface between the sacrum and the ilium of the hip bone

boreholes passages made by a drill for exploratory purposes

Byzantine Empire	the empire that ruled the eastern half of what was once the Roman Empire during the Middle Ages, with the capital city of Constantinople
context	how artifacts relate to each other and to their setting
Darwin, Charles	(1809–1882) an English naturalist, geologist, and biologist who is known for studies on evolution and the propagation of the idea that all species descend from common ancestors. It is said his restricted views on gender often reflected Victorian-era norms.
diaspora	the dispersion of people from their homeland
draft of a ship	the number of feet from the water line the deepest part of a boat or ship's hull is, or in other words, the depth of water needed to float a boat
epiphyseal union	loose secondary centers of bones that consist primarily of the joint portion of bone elements. The timing of epiphyseal union for different bone elements is well documented and helps when

trying to estimate the age of a young individual.

Eurasian Steppe the vast grassland and shrublands that stretch through Hungary; Bulgaria; Romania; Moldova; Ukraine; western Russia and Siberia; Kazakhstan; Xinjiang and Manchuria, China; and Mongolia that was traveled for trade; known as the Silk Road during the Middle Ages

excavate to carefully and systematically remove earth from an area in order to find artifacts and remains buried within

field research collecting and documenting archaeological data, including excavation and removal of objects

funeral pyre a construction where a body was placed (and lit together with things); needs not be the same as the grave

funereal a term used by archaeologists to describe something related to the treatment of the dead

garrison location of troops stationed in a fortress or town to defend it

grave goods	the things buried along with a person: personal possessions and/or things needed in the afterlife or things the family believes represent the person
greater sciatic notch	the larger of two openings in the posterior aspect of a hip bone
hillfort	a hilltop fortified with ramparts and ditches
human genome	genetic material contained in chromosomes that make up DNA
inhumation	a burial in the ground, whether in a trench of dirt, coffin, wooden chamber, or other method that leaves the body whole
Iron Age	time period in Scandinavia that began in approximately 500 BCE and lasted into the Viking Age, 1050 CE; called that because iron was the preferred metal for making tools
isotope analysis	taking a sample of bone tissue and converting it into a gas, then measuring its isotopic compositions (one of two or more types of atoms) with a device called a *mass spectrometer* that

separates the ions. These results can be compared between skeletal individuals to reveal the diet of the individuals as well as information about growth, stress, disease, and subsistence activities.

lið fighting units that were formed by chieftains and kings, the size of which depended on their wealth and influence. Warriors who signed up for these swore a bond of mutual loyalty to the cause of that campaign. When it was over, they broke up, and individuals returned home or joined another.

material culture artifacts in context: the tools, weapons, utensils, ornaments, art, monuments, structures, clothing, writings, religious images, and any other objects that humans have made

osteology the study of bones

Pavlovian skepticism skepticism toward or rejection of a fact because of prior conditioning to a different outcome

Pavlovian skepticism skepticism toward or rejection of a fact because of prior conditioning to a different outcome

preauricular sulcus	groove on the female pelvis that has been used as a common indicator of female sex of a skeleton; however, several studies have shown that this trait sometimes can be identified in skeletons of males, thus it is not in and of itself a clear indication for female sex. Even so, this groove is more common in females and they are also more likely to have a more distinct sulcus (i.e., broader/wider, deeper and longer than men).
Rus	initially the term for Scandinavians who visited and settled in what is now called Russia, it is thought to have derived from the Finnish word for a Swede, *Ruotsi*, or from the Greek term *rusioi*, which means people who are blond; also frequently used to describe the geographical area that is now Russia
Stone Age	a prehistoric period when stone or organic materials like bone, wood, and horn were used to make weapons and tools

DISCUSSION QUESTIONS

1. Stolpe was clearly a smart guy, and to his credit he brought stratigraphy to Scandinavian archaeology. Nonetheless, he suffered criticism from the Antiquities Academy for not being an archaeologist when the excavation began and was ridiculed for using one wrong word, "kitchen midden" (*kjökkenmödding*), when he meant garbage dump (*avskrädeshög*). Do you think his critics were justified in judging him so harshly? Why or why not?

2. When Stolpe opened a grave with substantial weapons and no "feminine" objects such as jewelry, he labeled it a "warrior grave." Today, archaeologists do not automatically assume a grave with weapons is a warrior. They label the grave a "weapons grave" until the full nature of the weapons and context can be explored. Do you agree or disagree with this change, and why? For what reasons other than warring might a person be buried with weapons?

3. Stolpe's records indicate that he used the term *he* or *male* to refer to the warrior in grave Bj 581. Price says, "I don't think he [Stolpe] ever really 'assessed' the sex. I don't think it was a decision at all. I don't think it occurred to anyone of that time that a person with those grave goods could be anything other than male." Do you think it was reasonable for Stolpe to assume the warrior was male, and if so, why do you think he did so?

4. Vikings are notoriously pictured in contemporary images wearing horned helmets. Scholars are unanimous in their view that Viking helmets did not have horns. What else can you think of in our culture today that misrepresents the Viking Age?

5. After performing morphological examinations on the bones from Bj 581, four separate, independent osteologists interpreted the person to be "very highly likely female" rather than merely "female." Why didn't they just say the person "is female"?

6. The field of archaeology has an established practice of announcing and commenting on research results through the peer-review process. Yet, many scholars in 2017 and 2019 chose to comment informally and through blog posts and other social media formats. Should they have taken the time and effort to write a peer-reviewed article? Would that have made their criticism more credible? What impact do you think social media is having on the scientific process? Is it good, bad, neither, or the wave of the future? What are the benefits of the peer-review process?

7. One of the criticisms of the team's research was that it set out to prove the person in Bj 581 was female. Anna Kjellström, Charlotte Hedenstierna-Jonson, and Neil Price vigorously disagreed. Price responded, "Were we interested? Of course. We're scientists. But one can't test DNA in such a way as to produce a desired result. It is what it is. We followed the trail of data and analysis." What do you think causes people to deny scientific facts, such as DNA results?

8. As is it often said by archaeologists, "The dead don't bury themselves." Thus, for the purpose of knowledge, archaeologists work with artifacts and settings that the deceased may not have selected and did not arrange. How do you imagine the survivors choose the grave goods?

9. Leszek Gardeła wrote that it was possible to access chamber graves long after the funeral, and this would have created

opportunities for all kinds of interactions between the living and the dead. It could include the removal, displacement, and even destruction of objects and bodies. Sometimes experts speculate that it was to establish supernatural contact with the deceased, to take out enchanted items such as family heirlooms, to bargain with the deceased to stay dead, or to perform magic or maim the dead—among other reasons. Why do you think Viking funerals and postdeath interactions were so intense?

10. Gender archaeologist Marianne Moen says, "We need to start thinking about [gender roles] as a bit more fluid and less strict and stop talking about men and women in different ways when they are buried the same way." What do you think she means when she says gender roles should be thought of as a bit more fluid? Why do you think she suggests this? Would it assist in minimizing gender bias and mistakes in interpretation?

11. Price and Moen suggest that the Vikings may have been gender fluid. What does this mean, and why might critics suggest this is at odds with other things we know about Viking culture?

12. In the Victorian period, archaeologists were biased in their beliefs about male and female gender roles and applied that bias to the Vikings. Today, scientists have DNA testing, and they know more about human karyotypes, intersex, transsexuality, and gender. When today's archaeologists say that the Vikings may have had a gender-fluid society, are they, like the Victorians, biased by current understandings? Is today's bias more defensible? Why or why not?

13. Assuming the team is correct that the person in Bj 581 presented as she/her on the gender spectrum, what might have caused her to live the life suggested by her grave goods?

14. What is your cultural bias? Do you think people of the Viking Age had the same social and cultural perspective that you do? In what way?

15. Assuming there are two archaeologists today from different cultures and they assess a Viking grave with different conclusions, do those conclusions have to be reconciled?

16. Our culture has exploded with images and characters based on Viking warrior women (shield-maidens). Why do you think female Viking warriors are so popular?

RESOURCES

THE ARTICLES AND THEIR SUPPLEMENTAL MATERIAL

Hedenstierna-Jonson, Charlotte, Anna Kjellström, Torun Zachrisson, Maja Krzewińska,Veronica Sobrado, Neil Price, Torsten Günther, Mattias Jakobsson, Anders Götherström, and Jan Storå. "A Female Viking Warrior Confirmed by Genomics." *American Journal of Physical Anthropology* 164, no. 4 (December 2017): 853–860. https://doi.org/10.1002/ajpa.23308.

Price, Neil, Charlotte Hedenstierna-Jonson, Torun Zachrisson, Anna Kjellström, Jan Storå, Maja Krzewińska, Torsten Günther, Verónica Sobrado, Mattias Jakobsson, and Anders Götherström. "Viking Warrior Women? Reassessing Birka Chamber Grave Bj.581." *Antiquity* 93, no. 367 (2019): 181–198. https://doi.org/10.15184/aqy.2018.258.

BOOKS FOR FURTHER STUDY

Arcini, Caroline Ahlström. *The Viking Age: A Time of Many Faces*. Oxford: Oxbow, 2018.

Brink, Stefan, and Neil Price, eds. *The Viking World*. New York: Routledge, 2012.

Brothwell, Don R. *Digging Up Bones: The Excavation, Treatment and Study of Human Skeletal Remains*. Ithaca, NY: Cornell University Press, 1981.

Chartrand, René, Keith Durham, Mark Harrison, and Ian Heath. *The Vikings: Voyagers of Discovery and Plunder*. New York: Osprey, 2006.

Fagan, Brian M., and Nadia Durrani. *In the Beginning: An Introduction to Archaeology*. 14th ed. New York: Routledge, 2020.

Findell, Martin. *Runes*. Los Angeles: J. Paul Getty Museum, 2014.

Gardeła, Leszek. *Women and Weapons in the Viking World: Amazons of the North*. Havertown, PA: Casemate, 2021.

Hjardar, Kim, and Vegard Vike. *Vikings at War*. Havertown, PA: Casemate, 2019.

Jesch, Judith. *The Viking Diaspora*. New York: Routledge, 2015.

Jesch, Judith. *Women in the Viking Age*. Rochester, NY: Boydell Press, 1991.

Price, Neil. *Children of Ash and Elm*. New York: Basic Books, 2020.

Price, Neil. *The Viking Way*. 2nd ed. Oxford: Oxbow Books, 2019.

Price, Neil and Stefan Brink, eds. *The Viking World*. 2nd ed. Routledge, 2012.

Pringle, Heather. "New Visions of the Vikings." *National Geographic*, March 2017.

Roesdahl, Else. *The Vikings*. 3rd ed. Translated by Susan M. Margeson and Kirsten Williams. London: Penguin, 2016.

ICELANDIC SAGAS AND POETRY

Egil's Saga. Translated by Bernard Scudder, with introduction and notes by Svanhildur Öskarsdóttir. New York: Penguin Classics, 1997.

Gisli Sursson's Saga and the Saga of the People of Eyri. Translated by Robert Cook, Terry Gunnell, Keneva Kunz, and Bernard Scudder. New York: Penguin Classics, 1997.

The Poetic Edda. Rev. ed. Translated by Carolyne Larrington. London: Oxford University Press, 2014.

The Sagas of the Icelanders. Translations by Andrew Wawn, Keneva Kunz, Terry Gunnell, Katrina C. Attwood, Anthony Maxwell, and George Clark. New York: Viking, 1997.

The Saga of the Volsungs with the Saga of Ragnar Lothbrok. Translated by Jackson Crawford. Indianapolis: Hackett, 2017.

Struluson, Snorri. *Edda*. Translated by Anthony Faulkes. London: Everyman, 1995.

The Vinland Sagas. Translated by Keneva Kunz. New York: Penguin Classics, 1997.

Viking Poetry of Love and War. Translated by Judith Jesch. London: British Museum, 2013.

WEBSITES AND ONLINE RESOURCES

Blogs

Jesch, Judith. "Let's Debate Female Viking Warriors Yet Again." *Norse and Viking Ramblings* (blog). September 9, 2017. http://norseandviking .blogspot.com/2017/09/lets-debate-female-viking-warriors-yet.html.

Jesch, Judith. "Some Further Discussion of the Article on Bj 581." *Norse and Viking Ramblings* (blog). September 18, 2017. http://norseandviking .blogspot.com/2017/09/some-further-discussion-of-article-on.html.

Jesch, Judith. "Viking Warrior Women—More of the Same? I." *Norse and Viking Ramblings* (blog). December 17, 2019. http://norseandviking .blogspot.com/2019/12/viking-warrior-women-more-of-same-i.html.

Jesch, Judith, "Viking Warrior Women—More of the Same? II." *Norse and Viking Ramblings* (blog). December 17, 2019. http://norseandviking .blogspot.com/2019/12/viking-warrior-women-more-of-same-ii.html.

Williams, Howard. "Viking Warrior Women: An *Archaeodeath* Response Part 1." *Archaeodeath* (blog). https://howardwilliamsblog.wordpress.com /2017/09/14/viking-warrior-women-an-archaeodeath-response-part-1/.

Websites

Stolpe, Hjalmar. Birka excavation drawings, notebooks, and diaries in manuscript. Twenty volumes plus six manuscripts and plans, stored in Antiquarian Topographical Archives in Stockholm, 1870–1888. Available at https://historiska.se/birka/digitala-resurser/.

Swedish History Museum. The Birka Portal. https://historiska.se/birka/.

Strömma Turism & Sjöfart AB. "The History of Birka, the Viking City." https://www.birkavikingastaden.se/en/about-birka/.

Film and Video

"The General Was Female?" *America's Hidden Stories.* Season 1, episode 6. The Smithsonian Channel, 2021.

Peiter, Sebastian. "Viking Warrior Women." Compact Media Group. Smithsonian docudrama. Features Anna Kjellström and Charlotte Hedenstierna-Jonson. 2020. https://www.imdb.com/title /tt10538348/?ref_=nm_knf_i1.

"Real Vikings E3 Viking Women." Features Charlotte Hedenstierna-Jonson, Neil Price, Anna Kjellström, and the actors from the History Channel's *Vikings* cast. YouTube, 41:58. https://www.youtube.com/watch?v= 4QNjglcwHp8.

"Secrets of the Vikings—Shield Maidens." History Channel. Neil Price shows the artwork with two armed women on a horse and the statue at the Danish Museum and discusses Bj 581. YouTube, 6:32. 2015. https:// www.youtube.com/watch?v=eUrq3aYuGOw.

"Viking Warrior Queen." *Secrets of the Dead*. July 7, 2020. PBS. Neil Price, Charlotte Hedenstierna-Jonson, and Anna Kjellström are interviewed. https://www.pbs.org/wnet/secrets/viking-warrior-queen/5180/.

The Viking Warrior Who Turned Out to Be a Woman. BBC, 2:50. March 17, 2021. https://www.bbc.com/reel/video/p099hyk0/the-viking -warrior-who-turned-out-to-be-a-woman.

Podcasts

Archaeology Podcast Network. https://www.archaeologypodcastnetwork .com.

Riddell, Fern. "Inghen Ruaidh, the Birka Grave and Viking Warrior Women," featuring Judith Jesch. September 14, 2020. *Not What You Thought You Knew*. https://play.acast.com/s/notwhatyouthought /inghenruaidh-thebirkagraveandvikingwarriorwomen.

MUSEUMS

Sweden

The Birka Museum
5, 178 92 Adelsö, Sweden
www.birkavikingastaden.se/en/

The Swedish History Museum
Narvavägen 13–17
114 84 Stockholm, Sweden
https://historiska.se/home/

Denmark
The National Museum of Denmark
Ny Vestergade 10, Prince's Mansion
DK-1471 København K, Denmark
https://en.natmus.dk/

Moesgaard Museum
Moesgård Allé 15
8270 Højbjerg, Denmark
www.moesgaardmuseum.dk

Norway
Oslo Viking Ship Museum
Huk Aveny 35
0287 Oslo, Norway
www.khm.uio.no

Lofotr Vikingmuseum
Prestegårdsveien 59, N-8360 Bøstad
https://www.lofotr.no/en/

Iceland
Viking World
Vikingabraut 1
260 Reykjanesbær, Iceland
https://www.vikingworld.is/#about

Finland
Rosala Viking Centre
Reimarsvägen 5
25950 Rosala, Finland
https://rosala.fi/en/museet/

Estonia
Viking Village
Saula, Kose Parish
75117 Harju County, Estonia

www.viikingitekyla.ee

United Kingdom
The British Museum
Great Russell St.
London WC1B 3DG, UK
www.britishmuseum.org

United States
The American Swedish Institute
2600 Park Ave.
Minneapolis, MN 55407
https://asimn.org/

National Nordic Museum
2655 NW Market Street
Seattle, WA 98107
https://nordicmuseum.org

NOTES

1. A REMARKABLE FIND: BIRKA, SWEDEN, 1878

"King of Birka": Bo G. Erikson, *Kungen av Birka: Hjalmar Stolpe Arkeolog och Etnograf* [King of Birka: Hjalmar Stolpe archaeologist and ethnographer] (Stockholm: Atlantis, 2015), 148–150. Selected pages here and throughout translated for author by Cynthia Wentland.

2. WHAT WE KNOW ABOUT THE VIKINGS

Viking Time Line: Portions of the Viking time line derived from "The Viking Time Line," The Viking Network, January 4, 2006, www.viking.no/e /etimeline.htm.

3. HJALMAR STOLPE: THE KING OF BIRKA AND HIS MOST FASCINATING FIND

"a small piece of amber!": Charlotte Hedenstierna-Jonson, "Hjalmar Stolpe (1841–1905)," in *Svenska Arkeologer*, ed. Anne-Sofie Gräslund (Uppsala, Sweden: Uppsala University, 2020), 47–52. Selected pages translated for author by Charlotte Hedenstierna-Jonson.

"a multitude of strangely cut beads": Erikson, *Kungen av Birka*, 31, 42.

"remnants of prehistoric living areas": Erikson, 46.

"I dug for two days": Erikson, 46.

"I must ask for a wool sweater": Erikson, 46.

"Only someone so inexperienced": Erikson, 52–54.

"I am convinced the only archaeology": Erikson, 54.

bone brushes and old toothbrushes: Erikson, 75.

"Instead of a more or less random": Erikson, 75.

"beads as well as fish bones": Erikson, 76.

"I investigate the whole mound": Erikson, 43.

"In the center of the chamber": Stolpe journals at the Swedish History Museum.

"Furthermore, it is clear": Leszek Gardeła, *Women and Weapons in the Viking World: Amazons of the North* (Havertown, PA: Casemate, 2021), 53.

"I am quick at playing chess": Gardeła, 53.

"perhaps the most remarkable grave": Neil Price et al., "Viking Warrior Women? Reassessing Birka Chamber Grave Bj.581," *Antiquity* 93, no. 367 (2019): 184, https://doi.org/10.15184/aqy.2018.258.

4. BIRKA TODAY

"Fortifications on land": Charlotte Hedenstierna-Jonson, "Women at War?: The Birka Female Warrior and Her Implications," in "New Horizons in the Archaeological Age," *SAArchaeological Record* 18, no. 3 (May 2018): 28.

"With great difficulty they accomplished": Rimbert, *Life of Anskar*, translated by Charles H. Robinson, chapter 11, accessed September 30, 2022, https://sourcebooks.fordham.edu/basis/anskar.asp#lifeans.

5. A CLOSER LOOK AT VIKING BONES BY OSTEOLOGISTS AND ARCHAEOLOGISTS

"Van der Merwe found a human": K. Kris Hirst, "Stable Isotope Analysis in Archaeology: Stable Isotopes and How the Research Works," ThoughtCo, October 9, 2018, https://www.thoughtco.com/stable-isotope-analysis-in-archaeology-172694.

6. OSTEOLOGISTS WEIGH IN ON THE BIRKA WARRIOR

"When I have them laid out": Anna Kjellström, in discussion with the author, March 4, 2021.

"I registered the bone": Kjellström, in discussion with the author.

"I examined every": Kjellström, in discussion with the author.

"I laid out the bones": Kjellström, in discussion with the author.

"The epiphyseal union": Kjellström, in discussion with the author.

"I knew it would be controversial": Kjellström, in discussion with the author.

"Another interesting (and possibly controversial)": Anna Kjellström, "People in Transition: Life in the Mälaren Valley from an Osteological Perspective," in *Shetland and the Viking World: Papers from the Proceedings of the 17th Viking Congress 2013*, ed. Val Turner (Lerwick, Scotland: Shetland Amenity Trust, 2017), 198.

7. WAIT! *WHAT?* THE FAMOUS BIRKA WARRIOR REALLY *IS* FEMALE!

"I think it is important to acknowledge": Charlotte Hedenstierna-Jonson, extended curriculum vitae provided to author.

"We all squatted and troweled": Hedenstierna-Jonson, in discussion with the author, April 21, 2020.

"We called each other": Hedenstierna-Jonson, in discussion with the author.

"Like most professional women do": Hedenstierna-Jonson, in discussion with the author.

"It refers to a person": Hedenstierna-Jonson, in discussion with the author.

"Of course, we wanted": Hedenstierna-Jonson, in discussion with the author.

"Anna, Torun, and I had our heads in our paperwork": Hedenstierna-Jonson, in discussion with the author.

"Objectives: The objective of this study": Charlotte Hedenstierna-Jonson et al., "A Female Viking Warrior Confirmed by Genomics," *American Journal of Physical Anthropology* 164, no. 4 (December 2017): 858. https://doi.org/10.1002/ajpa.23308.

"I called Neil Price": Hedenstierna-Jonson, in discussion with the author.

"When you find a woman": Sofia Lotto Persio, "Gender Reveal: Ancient Viking Warrior Was a Woman, DNA Analysis Shows," *Newsweek*, September 11, 2017, https://www.newsweek.com/gender-reveal-viking-warrior-was-woman-dna-analysis-show-662972.

"We are getting quite a lot": Paula Cocozza, "Does New DNA Evidence Prove That There Were Female Viking Warlords?" *Guardian*, September 12, 2017, https://www.theguardian.com/science/shortcuts/2017/sep/12/does-new-dna-evidence-prove-that-there-were-female-viking-warlords.

"Do weapons necessarily determine": Hedenstierna-Jonson et al., "A Female Viking Warrior Confirmed by Genomics," 858.

"generally dismissing women warriors": Hedenstierna-Jonson et al., "A Female
Viking Warrior Confirmed by Genomics," 853–860.

"generally mythological phenomenon": Judith Jesch, *Women in the Viking Age*
(Woodbridge, UK: Boydell Press, 1991), 182.

"What these examples": Judith Jesch, *The Viking Diaspora* (London: Routledge, 2015), 104.

"I completely concur": Fedir Androshchuk, "Female Viking Revisited," *Viking
and Medieval Scandinavia* 14 (2018): 47–60, https://doi.org
/10.1484/J.VMS.5.116389.

"Your skeleton can't tell us": Martin Rundkvist, "A Female Viking Warrior
Interred at Birka," *Aardvarchaeology* (blog), September 12, 2017,
https://aardvarchaeology.wordpress.com/2017/09/12/a-female-viking
-warrior-interred-at-birka/.

"Well, that's the key question": Michael Price, "Once This Viking Warrior Was
Revealed to Be a Woman, Some Began to Question Her Battle Bona
Fides," *Science*, September 14, 2017, https://www.science.org/content
/article/once-viking-warrior-was-revealed-be-woman-some-began
-question-her-battle-bona-fides.

8. WARRIORS, WEAPONS, AND WOMEN

"the warrior fled not": Judith Jesch, "Constructing the Warrior Ideal in the
Late Viking Age," in *The Martial Society: Aspects of Warriors, Fortifications, and Social Change in Scandinavia*, ed. Lena Holmquist Olausson
and Michael Olausson (Stockholm: Arch Research Lab, 2009).

"Sigmund owns this sack" through *"Things are bad"*: Neil Price, *Children of
Ash and Elm* (New York: Basic Books, 2020), 192.

"They [Harald's ships] were loaded": Price, 307–308.

"I went with bloody sword": Judith Jesch, trans., *Viking Poetry of Love and
War* (London: Trustees of the British Museum, 2013), 21.

"We have a big enough army": Kim Hjardar and Vegard Vike, *Vikings at War*,
Kindle ed. (Havertown, PA: Casemate (Ignition), 2016), 82.

Óðinn could bring it about": Snorri Sturluson, "Ynglinga Saga," trans. Alison
Finlay and Anthony Faukes, in *Heimskringla*, vol. 1 (University of Cambridge, 1951), 37.

"the term berserksgangr": Price, *Children of Ash and Elm*, 326.

"stock villains—useful antagonists": Price, 326.

"The Viking Age is known for": Caroline Ahlström Arcini, *The Viking Age*, Kindle ed. (Havertown, PA: Oxbow Books), 70, 85, 92–93.

"the slinger of the fire": Þórðr Særeksson (Sjáreksson), from his poem, "Þórálfs drápa Skólmssonar," 1 [Vol. 1], 237, kenning 5—a particularly long description.

"The ideal weapon almost came to life": Hjardar and Vike, *Vikings at War*, Kindle ed. (Havertown, PA: Casemate, 2016), 314.

"The effective use of Viking weaponry" and *"To use them"*: Price, *Children of Ash and Elm*, 300.

"The slimmest lances": Price, 302.

"Swords were slashing weapons": Price, 319.

"Today I started conservation": Vegard Vike (@VegardVike), Twitter, January 15, 2018, https://twitter.com/VegardVike/status /953052900737024000?cxt=HHwWgICwiYqk9rkaAAAA.

"The warp is woven": Robert Cook, trans., *Njal's Saga* (London: Penguin Classics, 1997).

"In a figurative sense": Jóhanna Katrín Friðriksdóttir, *Valkyrie: The Women of the Viking World* (London: Bloomsbury, 2021), 7.

"There were once women in Denmark": Judith Jesch, *Women in the Viking Age* (Boydell Press, 1991), 176.

"There is no doubt": Judith Jesch, in discussion with the author, June 8, 2021.

9. THE VIKING PHENOMENON AND THE TEAM'S FORMAL RESPONSE

"Rather embarrassingly, I was also": Neil Price, in discussion with the author, March 22, 2021.

"Rather than asking, What might this mean?": Price, in discussion with the author.

"It is important to remember": Price et al., "Viking Warrior Women?" 189.

"In short, there is nothing": Price et al., "Viking Warrior Women?" 181–198, and 12–13 of supplementary material.

"I still sometimes get questions like": Price, in discussion with the author.

"Can we be sure that the female-bodied": Price et al., "Viking Warrior Women?" 191.

"While we understand": Price et al., 191.

"Can we prove": Price et al., 192.

"Were we interested? Of course": Price, in discussion with the author.

"We must all be especially aware": Price, in discussion with the author.

"Currently, the figure": Price et al., "Viking Warrior Women?" 194.

"Which part of this person": Price, in discussion with the author.

"She adjusts and nuances": Price et al., "Viking Warrior Women?" 194.

"Instead, this is a case study": Price et al., 194.

"If Charlotte Hedenstierna-Jonson": Leszek Gardeła, *Women and Weapons in the Viking World: Amazons of the North* (Havertown, PA: Casemate, 2021), 55.

"We must still remain open": Gardeła's point that the lack of trauma should not be taken as evidence that the person had not been in combat is supported by Anna Kjellström: "A person making the argument that a lack of trauma is evidence of the person not being in battle suggests a lack of experience in osteoarchaeology. The individual in the grave may have been skilled/successful and not have received any injuries. The person may have suffered soft tissue injuries and died from these. The person may have suffered injuries that fractured bones that were destroyed postmortem—there are many elements missing from Bj 581." (Kjellström, in discussion with the author, August 23, 2021.)

"Grave disturbance was commonly practiced": Gardeła, 49.

"We have to acknowledge": Gardeła, 53, 54.

"Together with the rare silver hat": Gardeła, 55.

"It is quite possible that she was": Leszek Gardeła, in discussions with the author, April 26, 2021, and May 31, 2021.

10. FACE-TO-FACE WITH A BIRKA WARRIOR

"Your skeleton can't tell us": Rundkvist, "A Female Viking Warrior Interred," 1.

"an umbrella term for people": Harvard Medical School, "Foundational Concepts and Affirming Terminology Related to Sexual Orientation, Gender Identity, and Sex Development," last updated May 1, 2020, https://lgbt .hms.harvard.edu/terminology.

"how someone communicates": Harvard Medical School: Sexual and Gender Minority Health Equity Initiative, https://lgbt.hms.harvard.edu /files/lahms/files/terminology_guide_5.15.2020.pdf.

"diversity in sex characteristics": Harvard Medical School: Sexual and Gender

Minority Health Equity Initiative, https://lgbt.hms.harvard.edu
/files/lahms/files/terminology_guide_5.15.2020.pdf.

"Each year a portion of the population": Patricio Gargollo in discussion with
the author, August 4, 2021.

"A knife is an object": Marianne Moen, "Challenging Gender: A Reconsider-
ation of Gender in the Viking Age Using the Mortuary Landscape," PhD
Thesis 2019, 14.

"gender is of secondary importance": Marianne Moen, "No Man's Land or
Neutral Ground: Perceived Gendered Differences in Ideologies of War,"
Viking 84, no. 1 (November 19, 2021): 50.

"If gendered graves are used": Moen, "No Man's Land," 52.

"These include fixed beliefs": Moen, "No Man's Land," 56.

"We need to start thinking": Persio, "Gender Reveal: Ancient Viking Warrior
Was a Woman, DNA Analysis Shows," *Newsweek*, September 11, 2017.

"I saw one of them": Historynet, "Napoleonic Wars: Women at Waterloo,"
June 12, 2006, https://www.historynet.com/napoleonic-wars-women-at
-waterloo.htm.

"The individual could have been": Ulla Moilanen et al., "A Woman with a
Sword? Weapon Grave at Suontaka Vesitorninmäki, Finland," *European
Journal of Archaeology* 25, no. 1 (2022): 53, https://doi.org/http://dx.doi
.org/10.1017/eaa.2021.30. The authors emphasize the complexity of sex
and gender issues, how historically artifacts were viewed as binary male
or female, and how "some recent studies suggest that brains produce
personality, cognition, and behavior similarly regardless of chromosomal sex, in opposition to the idea that binary female and make differences exist in the brain.

"In a sense it does not": Price, *Children of Ash and Elm*, 177, 179.

"Every time we excavate a grave": Price, in discussion with the author.

"Beyond the obvious": Price, *Children of Ash and Elm*, 175.

"Not all burials conform": Price, *Children of Ash and Elm*, 178.

"This is a grave with": Price, in discussion with the author.

"If this woman actually was": "Viking Warrior Queen," *Secrets of the Dead*,
July 7, 2020, PBS. Neil Price, Charlotte Hedenstierna-Jonson, and Anna
Kjellström are interviewed, 2021, https://www.pbs.org/wnet
/secrets/viking-warrior-queen/5180/.

DISCUSSION QUESTIONS

"I don't think he": Price, in discussion with the author.

"Were we interested?": Price, in discussion with the author.

"We need to start": Persio, "Gender Reveal: Ancient Viking Warrior Was a Woman, DNA Analysis Shows," *Newsweek*, September 11, 2017.

INDEX

Note: Entries in italics refer to images.

175

176 INDEX

B

Battle of Clontarf, 102
Battle of Hafrsfjörðr, 89
Battle of Stamford Bridge, 7
berserkers, 89–92
bias, 141–142
Birka (Viking town), Sweden, 25
 artifacts and, 38, 39
 Bj 581 and, 26
 excavation of, 43–44
 Hedenstierna-Jonson and, 65–66, 69
 importance of, 6
 Kjellström and, 57
 rediscovery of, 14
 Stolpe and, 1
 Stolpe excavation and, 19–24
 trading and, 37–39
 warriors and, 40–41
Birka Museum, 134
Bj 581 (Viking gravesite)
 archaeological reactions to, 80–83
 bias and, 142
 bones in, 26, 60, 61
 discovery of, 1–4, 25
 drawing of, 4, 29
 Gardeła's reactions to, 123–129
 gender and, 119–120, 131–135,
  135, 146–148
 Hansen's engraving of, 28
 Hedenstierna-Jonson and, 67
 hnefatafl and, 31–32, 32
 horses and, 33
 Kjellström and, 64
 location of, 26
 Olsson's drawing of, 27
 osteology of bones and, 55–62
 other fragments and, 33, 34
 Price and, 115–118
 sex determination of bones and,
  62–64, 72–77
 similar gravesites and, 110–112
 Stolpe and, 15
 Viking burial practices and, 34–36
 weapons and, 30, 30
 women as warriors and, 122–123

Bj 854 femur, 58–59, 59, 117–118, 124
Björkö, Sweden, 1, 16–19, 16
Björköarätt (Law of Birka), 41
Black Death, 55
Black Earth, 18, 20, 37
Blad, Anders, 18
blockhouses, 37
Bloodaxe, Eric, 13
boat burials, 35, 94, 97
bone chemistry, 47–50
bones
 Atlas Project and, 71–73
 at Bj 581, 2–3, 26, 29
 Kjellström and, 55–62, 60
 osteology and, 45–50
 sex determination and, 50–52,
  62–64
 trauma to, 128
bowls, 127
bows and arrows, 98
Brannius, F. W., 18
British Museum, 113
burial mounds, 24, 35, 42, 43
burial practices, 34–36, 41, 46
Buried at Birka: Three Centuries, Four
 Viking Lives, 134
Byzantine Empire, 38, 71

C

Caliphate, 39
Canute the Great, 13
carbon 14 dating, 47–48
carbon isotopes, 47–48
Central Board of National Antiquities
 (Sweden), 18
children, 12, 88–90
Children of Ash and Elm (Price), 96,
 114, 146–147
China, 13
Christianity, 7, 87, 109
chromosomes, 132, 145–146